Liveness and Recording in the Media

Andrew Crisell

Professor of Broadcasting Studies, University of Sunderland, UK

First published 2012 by
PALGRAVE MACMILLAN

Palgrave Macmillan in the UK is an imprint of Macmillan Publishers Limited,
registered in England, company number 785998, of Houndmills, Basingstoke,
Hampshire RG21 6XS.

Palgrave Macmillan in the US is a division of St Martin's Press LLC,
175 Fifth Avenue, New York, NY 10010.

Palgrave Macmillan is the global academic imprint of the above companies
and has companies and representatives throughout the world.

Palgrave® and Macmillan® are registered trademarks in the United States,
the United Kingdom, Europe and other countries

ISBN-13: 978–0–230–28222–3

This book is printed on paper suitable for recycling and made from fully
managed and sustained forest sources. Logging, pulping and manufacturing
processes are expected to conform to the environmental regulations of the
country of origin.

A catalogue record for this book is available from the British Library.

A catalog record for this book is available from the Library of Congress.

10   9   8   7   6   5   4   3   2   1
21   20   19   18   17   16   15   14   13   12

Printed and bound in Great Britain by
CPI Antony Rowe, Chippenham and Eastbourne

To my grandson Milo Manson,
perhaps the livest creature on the planet

Contents

Preface

In the course of this book I have been wilfully inconsistent in referring to broadcasting – radio and television – sometimes, and punctiliously, as 'media' and sometimes, more loosely, as 'a medium'. This is because at certain points I have been concerned to acknowledge the sense in which radio and television differ, while at others to stress the mostly deeper things they have in common. However I am confident that the context will obviate any confusion in the mind of the reader. Moreover, since my concern for the reader's well-being is even greater than my fear of the gender police, I have tried not to vex her/him with such ponderous dualisms as 'she/he' but where I have wished to consider the viewer, newsreader and so on as a single individual, have freely referred to her/him as 'she/her' in one place and 'he/him' in another, with the intention that where one gender is made explicit, the other is always implied.

Acknowledgements

The readers of a book of this kind might assume that the author's family and close colleagues have been his main source of inspiration and assistance, and in my case they are right. At the University of Sunderland, I am particularly indebted to three colleagues in the Department of Media and Cultural Studies whom I also regard as good friends. Shaun Moores, Professor of Media and Communications, drew my attention to a number of important books and articles on liveness in the media and also provided stimulating conversation on the subject. Rob Jewitt was a source of great insight into the arcana of file-sharing, music websites and the downloading of film rentals in a way that allows viewing yet prevents retention. And with the unfailing patience and cheerfulness for which he is renowned, Peter Burt, former chief technician in the department, recorded for me a whole evening's television programmes on BBC 1.

Certain members of my family are so knowledgeable about media technologies and the practices of broadcasting institutions that I sometimes feel I have less right than any of them to claim expertise in the field. As in the writing of my previous books, I am grateful to my brother-in-law Tony Humphreys for his painstaking researches into Netflix and other film-streaming services and his helpful explanations of how new media technologies work. My older daughter Ellie was a source of information about the prioritisation and scheduling of stories in television rolling news, and without a lucid account of proprietary music websites from my younger daughter Hattie, I might have assumed that 'Spotify' was a treatment for dermatological disorders.

However, none of these good friends and relatives must suffer from guilt by association, for the reader should be clear that the errors, omissions and perversities of opinion that she might encounter in this book belong only to me.

Introduction:
The Scope of the Book

The purpose of this book is to address a familiar paradox that has never-theless received little scholarly attention. Why should radio and televi-sion, whose great innovation was to introduce liveness to mass communication, and which even today make something of a fetish of this quality, carry so much material that is *not* live? And why should they then pretend for the most part that it *is* live? The paradox may not require lengthy treatment but is certainly worth considering in a series that covers the 'topical' media of radio, television and newspapers and addresses their key concerns in respect of technologies, institutions, content, conventions and contexts. Moreover while the explanation is at one level straightforward, it is at another rather less so and prompts some interesting speculations. Given the obvious limitations of live communication, why for instance does it seem so persistently relevant? Can we consider the other modes of communication to be self-sufficient, or are they always in some sense aspiring or surrogate versions of the live mode?

For reasons that are self-evident the focus of the book is on broad-casting – radio and television – but in the chapter on radio there is much discussion of liveness and recording in *music*, and this requires an explanation. Music is sometimes described as a 'medium' but it is clearly not one in the same sense as the radio, television or the newspaper and, notwithstanding the complicating impact of new technologies, these three media form the series' main area of attention. Music is diffused – that is, played and sometimes sold – not just through broadcasting but in shops and on the internet. However, it has had a close relationship with radio throughout the latter's history and especially since television stole so much of its content and its audience. As we might expect, music throws an interesting light on the relationship between liveness and recording, but I wish to argue that it also illuminates some central philosophical issues about the nature and purposes of broadcasting. Adopting Sylvia Harvey's helpful categorisations, it is possible to see broadcasting as an expression either of 'communicative rights' on the one hand or 'market freedom' on the other (Harvey, 2002, p. 220). The former, essentially a public-service position, can be taken to imply that radio and television should as far as possible diffuse material that has been hitherto unavailable to the great mass of people or which they would find impossible or difficult to access by other means. The latter philosophy regards these media simply as vehicles for the promotion and sale of products and services. My somewhat tentative suggestion in this book is that following almost fifty years during which radio has largely given itself over to recorded music, and thus reflected a market philosophy which the BBC has adopted as much as any other broadcaster, new technology may bring about a return to radio of live or as-live music for the primary purpose of performance rather than promotion, and thus provide a belated vindication of the old public-service ideal.

The examples I have used to illustrate particular aspects of liveness and recording have been drawn almost entirely from British broadcasting. My excuse is that, having embraced for nearly sixty years both a major public-service broadcaster, the BBC, and a thriving commercial sector, the British system provides a useful microcosm of the kinds of broadcasting that exist elsewhere in the world. I hope, then, that my examples will be recognisable to students of all nationalities.

1 Liveness and Broadcasting

Liveness has always been associated with broadcasting – radio and television – because the mass media that preceded it were recorded. In order to convey their messages, print, photography, sound reproduction and cinema each made use of some form of carrier or 'text', but the messages of broadcasting are sent over the air, are received in the same instant, and then cease to exist. We might nevertheless be reluctant to define broadcasting in terms of liveness because so much of it is plainly *not* live. Many radio and television programmes are created before they are transmitted and, whether or not they are pre-recorded in this way, are not consumed at the time they are transmitted. Even substantially live programmes such as news bulletins are punctuated with pre-recorded inserts. Nor is the use of pre-recorded content the effect of new technology, for television was able to carry filmed material from its very beginnings (Ellis, 2002, p. 31).

The awkwardness of the concept of liveness might therefore encourage us to define broadcasting in terms of certain of its other characteristics. One is that radio and television have for the most part been consumed *privately* – by individuals or small groups in their homes or other 'owned' spaces such as cars or rooms in hotels and hostels. The older media of theatre and cinema required their audiences to gather in public venues, and it is convenient to see broadcasting as part of that great movement towards an individualism of ownership and consumption that has developed over the last 100 years and more. The motor car, computers and the internet, and now mobile telephony have enabled us to fulfil our professional duties, domestic chores, financial and shopping needs and cultural interests increasingly in accordance with our own wishes and free of the need to enter the public sphere or observe such external constraints as bus and train timetables or hours of business (Crisell, 2002, pp. 9–10). Moreover broadcasting has smoothly absorbed the older and public media and turned them into private ones: radio and television domesticated the theatre and television domesticated the cinema. We will see shortly that this has had a huge impact

1

on broadcasting by forcing it not only to rely heavily on pre-recorded material but to make extensive use of certain cultural forms which it did not originate but which have come to be pre-eminently associated with it.

Nevertheless it is not altogether helpful to define broadcasting primarily in terms of the privacy or domesticity of its consumption because this may also characterise the consumption of books and newspapers, not to mention newer media such as the internet. Moreover, the first experiences of television were public. This is perhaps because while radio sets have been relatively cheap to buy or make throughout the history of sound broadcasting, the initial cost of television receivers was expected to be beyond the pockets of all but a few. Baird's first demonstration of his new device took place in Selfridges department store in 1925, and the world's first regular television service, which was launched in Germany in March 1935, was beamed only to public auditoria: there were no privately owned sets (Chapman, 2005, p. 117). The British television service was started by the BBC in November 1936, but the first receivers cost almost as much as a car and many of its programmes were viewed in shops, cinemas and other public places (Ellis, 2002, p. 31). By 1937, there were as many as 109 public viewing rooms, including one at Harrods and one at Waterloo railway station (Gripsrud, 1998, p. 22). We think of modern television as a predominantly domestic and private medium, but it is worth remembering that a significant proportion of the audience continues to watch its programmes, especially major sporting events, in pubs and clubs, not to mention open spaces like town squares and stadiums.

Despite all the problems that the concept presents, we persist in feeling that *liveness* is the distinguishing feature of broadcasting. But what, exactly, does 'live' mean?

2 The Meaning of 'Live'

The phenomenon of liveness is unexpectedly complicated, and it is perhaps an awareness of this and not merely of the fact that in most broadcasting, liveness and recordedness are thoroughly intermingled, that has tempted some scholars to seek to define broadcasting in terms of other characteristics. Let us begin by imagining a simple instance of a live act of communication: two people within a single space, one of whom is talking to the other. They are face to face. What is being communicated by one is being directly and simultaneously apprehended by the other. The latter hears the words of the former, but he can also see her facial expressions, gestures and posture. The speaker may also enhance the communication by using touch, placing her hand on the listener's arm or his shoulder. We can also say that these two people have no need of a *medium* through which to communicate, though even this assertion needs to be qualified for it could be argued that *all* communication requires a medium – needs, in other words, to be 'mediated'. The medium in this simple instance of *interpersonal* communication – that is, communication between two or more people – is made up of their physical faculties: the lungs, vocal cords, speech and overall comportment of the speaker, and the sight, hearing and sense of touch of the listener. However, for the sake of clarity and convenience, we can assert that these two people have no need of a medium in the sense that they require no artificial or technological enhancement of the communication that is taking place between them. It is 'unmediated' and thus literally *immediate*, a word that mostly assumes a temporal meaning but which here also has a spatial dimension. (Our notions of time and space are in any case closely bound up with each other, a fact that will no doubt become apparent in the discussion that follows.) We might now suggest that a *live* communication takes place when the author of a message is also her own medium.

Let us imagine another act of communication, one that will be familiar to many of us: a lecturer is addressing an auditorium full of students.

If she is speaking to a large number of them yet thanks to her own powers of delivery and the acoustic quality of the auditorium has no need of a microphone, we might stretch a point and describe her lecture as a form of mass communication (the boundary between 'personal' and 'mass' communication has never been clearly defined) which is unmediated. Over distances – that is, beyond the point at which our physical faculties can be deployed – communication must become *mediated*: it requires a medium. This medium might be handwriting and take the form of a letter; or it might be 'mechanised' writing or print and take the form of a newspaper, book or journal; or it might consist of mechanically reproduced images in the form of a film. However, because of the distances involved, some of them considerable, a time lapse occurs while such communications (in the interests of simplicity we can just call them 'messages') are conveyed by *intermediaries*: typically, the Post Office in the case of letters; booksellers and newsagents in the case of printed messages, but also several other intermediaries such as printers and publishers; and chains of cinemas in the case of films. The great innovation of broadcasting was to convey messages over distances *without the time lapse*, and this is the basis of its claim to liveness.

It is worth pondering this innovation for a moment. At the turn of the twentieth century and for the first time in history, broadcasting (perhaps we should use the term 'telecommunication' since it applies to telephony too) created an uncoupling of space and time in the sense that movement across distances no longer involved delay: 'the same time' no longer presupposed 'the same space' (Thompson, 1995, p. 32). What broadcasting recreates is that original, ideal form of instantaneous communication that we outlined at the beginning of this chapter. A medium is, of course, involved because though co-present in time, the sender of the communication and the receiver of it are separate in space. As Paddy Scannell observes, broadcasting creates 'new possibilities of being: of being in two places at once' (Scannell, 1996, p. 91) and so, to stand words on their head, broadcasting is an 'immediate medium': whether in the form of radio or television, there is an element of self-effacement about it. Indeed, there are three respects in which radio and television present their content as if it were immediate. First, the technological advances that they embody have quickened the pace of communication and improved quality by eliminating 'noise', those non-meaningful elements of the communication such as electrical interference. Second, and in the coverage of live events like news, sport and concerts, there is a goal of immediacy among broadcasting professionals.

Third, telemedia are presented to us as if on equal ontological terms with our own sensory faculties: in other words the experiences they convey seem to be on a par with, sometimes even to be indistinguishable from, our first-hand experiences (Tomlinson, 2007, pp. 99–101).

Broadcasting is live, then, in the sense that, as with face-to-face communication, its messages are received at the instant they are sent. Yet liveness remains a tricky concept, as in the following imaginary instances:

1   You are a medieval monarch and a messenger brings you a verbal message from another monarch. He stands before you, genuflects and bows low, kisses your hand, looks you in the eye and utters the message. Is this a live communication? Most of us, perhaps, would say that it was not, because while it has all the trappings of liveness, the message was authored by another person who is absent. So the speaker standing before you is a mere medium.

Now let us consider three more instances:

2   You are watching a television news bulletin. The newsreader is addressing the camera directly and because the item concerns your favourite football team you are paying close attention to her words. But she has not drafted any of them. Is the communication live?
3   I am giving a lecture, every word of which is my own, but I wrote it last week. Is the communication live?
4   We are sitting in a theatre and watching a play. The actors are physically present before us and speaking to us, or at least for our benefit. We can smell their grease-paint and even the smoke effects from a battle scene that has just taken place. The actors are delivering their lines to each other, and from time to time one of them even addresses us directly in the form of a soliloquy. But the lines were written by a playwright who is absent and, as in the case of Shakespeare, may even have been dead for several hundred years. Is the communication live?

It is possible to assert that none of these communications is live: at the very least, they illustrate that liveness and 'recordedness' alternate and intermingle much more frequently than we might suppose. The newsreader is merely a part of the medium and, as a lecturer, I am merely the medium for myself as a writer. Similarly, the actors are merely purveyors or 'media' of a message written by the playwright. This example of the play is perhaps the most disconcerting, for theatre is invariably lauded for its liveness, especially in comparison with cinema (and curiously enough, television: more on this in a moment).

Perhaps the best answer we can devise is that it all depends on whom we regard as the author or originator of these communications. In each of them we could argue that the speakers inevitably contribute something of their own to the communication through 'paralinguistic' factors – all those factors outside the actual words, such as intonation, pitch and speed of speaking, pauses, gesture, facial expression and posture which help to 'realise' it, to bridge the gap between the words as they occur on the page or in the script and what is understood by the audience. In the case of the news bulletin, is the author the person who wrote the copy, or 'the broadcasting institution', or the newsreader as some kind of symbol or embodiment of the institution? In the case of our newsreader or royal messenger we might indeed take a more collective view of authorship or origination, seeing them as the personification of the organisation or state that they represent, whether it be the BBC or the Holy Roman Empire. In the case of our play, it is helpful to remember that what the dramatist writes is nothing more than a *blueprint* for performance: the actors do so much to contribute to the final artistic effect that we might perceive them as co-authors. To affirm, for example, that no two productions of Shakespeare are alike is to concede the varying creative contributions that different companies of actors make to the playwright's original text.

Unfortunately, however, we have not quite dealt with all the trickiness that bedevils the concept of liveness. We have implied that each of the above forms of communication can be treated as live because there is no absolute distinction between those who are delivering the communication and those who have originated it. But it is also possible to object that radio and television can *never* be live because however self-effacing they may be, they are media and thus offer *mediated* communication: they may provide co-presence in time but they cannot provide co-presence in space, the second aspect of liveness that characterised our very first example of live communication. This objection is by no means trivial: it is what people mean when they say that they prefer the live entertainment of the theatre to watching television. Even at an academic level 'mediated' may be opposed or contrasted to 'live', if only implicitly and intermittently (see, for example, Auslander, 1999, pp. 1, 2, 7).

Nevertheless for our discussion of broadcasting we will adopt the narrower if more widely accepted understanding of liveness: that all broadcast content is live in the sense that everything that radio and television stations transmit is received, or is capable of being received, at the moment it is transmitted. At the very least, this understanding of liveness explains why television is usually thought of as being nearer to theatre than to cinema (Auslander, 1999, p. 12).

3 What's So Special about Liveness?

Yet why is liveness to be aspired to? Why have I presumed to talk about face-to-face communication as the 'ideal' form that broadcasting seeks to recreate? I am not alone in so doing because most linguisticians treat conversation as the normal, prototypical form of language usage against which mediated forms of talk are studied for their 'deviations' (Scannell, 1991, pp. 11–12). Nevertheless its use as an ideal or benchmark for all other modes of communication seems to be open to some formidable objections.

Let us compare it with the oldest of technologies for recording communication, writing, which was in existence for several thousand years before it became mechanised at the end of the fifteenth century, and in that form is known as *print*. For the most part, writing differs from sound recording in being not a transcript, a record or recording of what has already been said, but a record of what the originator of the communication wishes to say *in the best possible way* – that is, in the clearest, most informative, most persuasive, most moving, beststructured way, depending of course on the nature and purpose of the communication. Without the technologies of writing and printing – the ability to fix symbols, whether words, figures or other marks, on a medium such as paper or parchment – most of the philosophical, scientific, literary, artistic and political achievements of advanced civilisation would have been impossible. Intellectual activity could not have developed beyond the narrow compass of the human memory and, for this reason, writing is not only a prerequisite of computers and information technology but was far more momentous than they are (Ong, 1982, p. 82).

Precisely because writing and printing are for the most part not direct recordings of speech in the sense that sound reproduction is – because they seem to involve premeditation to a much greater extent – we would expect them to have travelled a long way from the typical idioms of speech. To compensate for the ephemeral, imprecise, untidy, repetitive, incoherent and context-dependent character of much speech, we have developed a literary culture over hundreds of years, most noticeably in those fields of writing which focus on intellectual matters: ideas, theories and analyses. We are therefore able to speak of 'literary idioms' and 'literary register', features of language which relate to words and syntax and are much more typical of writing and print than of conventional extemporised speech.

Since it is hard to think of a subject that is likely to be drier, more intellectual and more 'literary' than philosophy, let us consider the following passage from a study of the German philosopher Immanuel Kant (1724–1804):

Whatever we may think of the validity of the inference to the subjectivity of a notion from its *a priori* character, Kant does hold that the *a priori* forms of perception are also subjective; and that we consequently cannot perceive the world as it is. We change it by perceiving it. This being so the question arises whether space and time, being subjective forms, are real or – what seems to be a philosophically preferable way to put it – in what sense they are real and in what sense they are not.

Space, it follows from the Kantian analysis, is empirically real; that is to say, it is real 'with respect to everything which can be given to us as an external object'. It is also transcendentally ideal; which means, in Kantian nomenclature, that 'with respect to things ... considered in themselves' space is not real. Time, too, in which all perceptions are situated, is empirically real, that is to say it is real 'with respect to all objects which could ever be given to our senses' and it is transcendentally ideal. 'Once we abstract from the subjective conditions of perception it is nothing at all and cannot be attributed to the things in themselves.'

(Stefan Körner, *Kant*, Yale University Press, 1955)

The literary features of this passage, by which we mean features that are much more likely to occur in writing than in speech (many features are, of course, common to both), are all too obvious. Many of the more literary words have a tendency to abstraction, and any list of them would probably include *inference, subjectivity, a priori, perceive* (as distinct from merely 'see'), *empirically* and *transcendentally*. In the case of *nomenclature*, a system of names, we might even be uncertain as to how it is meant to be pronounced, for where does the stress lie – on the first or second or third syllable? (*The Oxford Dictionary of English* tells us it should lie on the first, which leaves an unusually large number of unstressed syllables – three – in its wake.)

It is highly likely that if this passage were read aloud to us we would be unable to make much sense of it, particularly at first hearing. It is intended for the eyes rather than the ears and might therefore be described as 'readerly'. And yet I would suggest that, even in such a communication as this, there is a hankering after liveness, a need on the part of the writer, however obscurely felt, to invest it with some modicum of the personal. I would also suggest that it is a need that seldom disappears entirely from written language. One feature of the language whose effect is to depersonalise actions and which our literary culture is therefore likely to have encouraged is the passive form of the verb. It replaces the active form, as in the phrase 'He *stole* the book', with 'The book *was stolen*', thus leaving the perpetrator of the action usefully indeterminate. In the above passage there are places where the writer could have chosen this passive form: 'Whatever might be thought of the validity ...'; 'the world cannot be perceived as it is', but in fact the writing is a little more personal: 'Whatever *we* may think ...'; '*we* [...] cannot perceive the world as it is'.

Who is this 'we'? As is common with personal pronouns, its field of reference seems to vary slightly. In the second of these two uses and in the subsequent occurrences of 'we' and its related forms 'our' and 'us', all of these within quotations from Kant himself, the reference is to our collective experience as human beings, and its use is thus not especially personal. But the first use of the pronoun ('Whatever we may think ...') is the writer's and evidently refers only to himself and the reader: he prefers to think of himself not as delivering a monologue – as the 'owner' of the communication, which, strictly speaking, he is – but as engaged in a conversation, in a collaborative effort to appraise Kant's thought.

There are certain other ways in which the writing seems to aspire to liveness. The writer speculates about whether space and time are real but then, in a manner more characteristic of speech than writing, checks himself and modifies his thought: 'or – what seems to be a philosophically preferable way to put it – in what sense they are real ...'. This process is quintessentially temporal: the unfolding of a thought and the self-correction are what goes on in time, and because we tend to think of writing as a static, finished product, its usual function is to record the outcome of the process rather than the process itself. In the second paragraph of the passage there is another modification of a thought, or more accurately a gloss on it: 'that is to say'. The writer does not, as he more logically could, write 'that is to write', and this is because he thinks of his reader as co-present – not so much a reader as a listener, and thus of himself as a *speaker*. Sometimes writing craves co-presence as much as speech does: even in this dry, cerebral passage we can detect a kind of metalingual yearning to step out of the limitations of the medium and ensure that the receiver of the message is keeping up with its originator, something that writing, non-live communication, can never actually do. There is a sense in which writing, for all its intellectual and emotional potential, is not so much an enhancement of speech as an inadequate substitute for it.

What, then, is so special about liveness? It has been shrewdly observed that before the possibility of recording, liveness had no significance because *all* communication was live (Auslander, 1999, p. 54). Only within a world that is largely characterised by different kinds of recorded communication, of which writing and printing are probably the commonest, do its virtues become evident. Our philosophical writer craves a co-presence with the reader because he wishes to check that the latter is receiving and understanding his message, and in so doing he is harking back to what we might term the default position or benchmark of all communication: the face-to-face mode. It is this mode that most if not all the other media either derive from or seek to recreate. Our writer thinks of talking and being heard as a useful way of denying, or at least disguising, the separation and absence that are involved in the medium he is obliged to adopt.

We can say two more things about the passage. First, the need for co-presence is primarily felt by the writer rather than the reader, though by allowing a fuller understanding and the opportunity of feedback, co-presence would of course benefit both parties. Second, it is primarily a need for co-presence in space, though of course temporal co-presence is a concomitant of it. This craving for co-presence must also explain why people continue to go to the theatre when cinema is available, and why some *prefer* it to the cinema even though its disadvantages are manifold. Let us remind ourselves of some of these. First, in comparison with the cinema, theatre affords a relatively distant or reduced view of the dramatic performance, even to those who are sitting at the front of the auditorium. Second, in a live performance there is always the risk that one or more of the actors will be below their best, forget lines or miscue. Third, there is a possibility, stronger for those sitting further back in the auditorium, that some of the dialogue will be inaudible. And fourth, theatrical sets are limited in scope and obviously artificial, if only in their lack of a 'fourth wall'.

Theatre lovers will insist that the spontaneity of the performance, the element of liveness that involves suddenness and unpredictability, outweighs these disadvantages, along with the existence of a two-way relationship – most palpable in comedy – which enables the audience to influence the actors through laughter, rapt silence, applause and so on. This relationship is, of course, impossible in the cinema. Again, there are two things about it which are worth remembering. First, while co-presence benefits both parties by allowing the 'senders' of the theatrical communication to be influenced for the better by the receivers, the need for co-presence is primarily felt by the receivers rather than the senders. The basis for this assertion is that cinematic actors are often able to perform very effectively even though they lack a co-present audience. Second, and as we observed when discussing the philosophical passage, the need is primarily for a co-presence in space, even though temporal co-presence is bound up with it.

However, the desire for liveness which is shared by our philosophical writer and our theatrical audience would not be satisfied by the liveness that characterises broadcasting. Like cinema, broadcasting does not suffer from the poor visibility and audibility that limit the theatre, nor from the artificiality of its sets and settings, but neither of course can it offer the two-way relationship of the theatre – an opportunity to the audience to influence the senders of its messages. The problem is that, although co-present in time, the sender and receivers of broadcast messages are not co-present in space: indeed, and as we have already seen, it is for just this reason that some people have felt that radio and television are *not* live media. Thus whatever case we can make for broadcasting's liveness must be based on the purely temporal co-presence it offers, the need for which is primarily felt by the receivers rather than the senders of its messages.

What, then, are the advantages conferred by broadcasting's liveness? The two most obvious are that its messages are up to date and also, in affording less opportunity for deception, more likely to be truthful than other kinds of messages. One thing we can be certain of with any kind of recording, whether visual or auditory, is that things will have happened since it was made. The temporal co-presence on which broadcasting's liveness is based therefore makes both television and radio especially useful as news media – diffusers of messages that are time-sensitive in the sense that the events they report are both *recent* and *ephemeral*. Events that are not recent are historical and of no news value, but newsworthy events also tend to win our attention for just a short time, if only because they must yield to 'newer' ones. Typically they occur within the fields of politics and current affairs, the national economy, cultural activity and showbusiness, or that broad area of experience to which we can all relate and which gives them the title of 'human-interest' stories. It is hardly surprising that in the UK, the Newspaper Proprietors' Association immediately feared radio's ability to transmit the news instantaneously and successfully lobbied the government to restrict both the amount it could broadcast and the sources it could access. These restrictions persisted from radio's birth in 1922 until 1938, when the approach of war meant that vested interests could no longer be allowed to prevent news from being disseminated as swiftly as possible (Crisell, 2002, p. 33).

A form of news that is especially suited to the liveness of broadcasting is sport because, unlike theatre and most other forms of entertainment, sporting occasions have an unknown outcome. This helps to explain why they are almost uniquely able to disrupt broadcasting schedules, displacing even the other and often more 'serious' news transmissions, and why they are able to win and hold very large audiences outside conventional peak viewing times (Whannel, 1992, p. 93).

Given television's and radio's especial strengths as news media, it is not surprising that we also value the liveness of broadcasting for its truthfulness and authenticity. In our 'benchmark' mode of communication – face to face – it is harder for a speaker to deceive a listener than if, for instance, she were writing to him. Liveness implies reality in the raw and thus an inability to lie (Gripsrud, 1998, p. 20). It is spontaneous, uncontrollable and free of editorial interference. We can illuminate this point with another glance at history. Before the Second World War, the great fear of the government was that broadcasting could be used to make seditious or politically inflammatory remarks. Because print is a recorded medium, because, between the expression of a remark and its reception by readers, there is a time lapse which allows intervention, the newspapers were considered not to pose quite such a threat. The BBC therefore sought to appease the government by ensuring that there would be no 'reality in the raw': virtually all broadcast speech was pre-scripted.

We might think that this is no longer an issue between government and broadcasters, but we would be wrong. Unless they are ongoing, many of the newsworthy events that are covered by broadcasting have to be recorded or reported rather than transmitted live. Hence, in order to exploit the character of the medium, it will often provide the next best thing: live, spontaneous reactions to these events instead of rehearsed or scripted ones. In May 2003, the BBC's defence correspondent, Andrew Gilligan, asserted during an unscripted interview by John Humphrys on Radio 4's *Today* programme that, in its newly published report on Iraq's weapons of mass destruction, the government made what it knew was the untrue claim that they could be mobilised within forty-five minutes. Led by Alastair Campbell, its chief spin doctor and the main author of the report, the government angrily denied the charge. The repercussions were enormous and included the apparent suicide of the government scientist who had secretly briefed Gilligan and a report by Lord Hutton which censured both Gilligan and the BBC. In asserting that Gilligan's words should have been scripted and vetted, the report revealed both a legalistic and political desire for premeditated and evidentially precise texts and a refusal, wilful or otherwise, to appreciate that broadcasting, being live, exists to convey the impromptu, the improvised and the unpredictable (Montgomery, 2006). Hence the Gilligan affair shows that governments still fear broadcasting's liveness because of its relative freedom from editorial control. The live nature of Gilligan's remarks does not, of course, necessarily mean that they were a truthful account of what the government had done, but they do seem to have been an honest expression of what he *thought* it had done.

However, there seems to be a deeper human need for liveness – one which unites our solitary philosophical writer with the avid radio listener and television viewer and even the gregarious theatregoer. Let us begin by reminding ourselves that the crucial element of liveness is temporal: co-presence in *time*. If we accept that broadcasting can be live, as we have in this book, then co-presence in *space* is merely optional. Co-presence in space without temporal co-presence is almost meaningless because if two people are not temporally co-present they cannot be spatially co-present. If I were to claim co-presence with King Charles I because I am standing on the very spot from which he addressed his executioners in 1649, I would be stretching the term beyond breaking point. Hence if the crucial element of liveness is existence in time, it follows that the most interesting objects of live coverage are those that manifest the process of temporal existence, for instance by moving or making noises. They should, in other words, be living. This explains why the words *alive* ('possessing life') and *live* ('conveying presence') can sometimes be hard to distinguish.

It is, of course, possible to have live television transmissions of things that are not alive – the 'still life' of a statue or bowl of fruit – and some of the experimental broadcasts of John Logie Baird and others did just this. But what is the point of televising something from another location if you cannot also show that it is alive, inhabiting the same time as the viewer? For nearly all of us, the most interesting living things are other humans, but even if what we see on the television are merely inanimate objects or animals, they will be made intelligible or interesting to us only by a human presence. The human may be invisible to us – simply a 'voiceover'. She may be entirely focused on the objects or animals we can see and provide little more than voiced captions. But it is notable that television almost never provides *written* captions in this context: we are interested in these things only as they are filtered through the intelligence of another living person.

This point becomes even clearer when we consider radio. On radio, the only reality is sound: if something cannot be heard, it doesn't exist. Hence the still life that could be transmitted on television would be impossible on the radio. Nevertheless, sounds *per se* are either hard to identify or of uncertain significance. Is the purring machinery that I can hear an electric fan or a vacuum cleaner or a hairdryer? And while I'm sure that I can hear the crash of waves, do these signify a documentary about the fishing industry or a thriller about a shipwreck? These sounds need the contextualisation provided by words, and on the radio these must be *spoken* words – sounds made by humans (Crisell, 1994, pp. 44–8, 53–5). What we want from broadcast liveness, then, is essentially the co-presence of other humans, either as objects of interest in themselves or as a way of making what is non-human intelligible and interesting to us. But I would want to go further and argue that our love of liveness is essentially a desire for the company of other humans which is separate from, and antecedent to, anything they might have to say to us or we to them.

The evidence for this is fragmentary and elusive but still, perhaps, cogent. Let us look first at music radio. Unlike many other non-verbal sounds, music on the radio is always and instantly recognisable for what it is, and the significance of it, if such a term is appropriate, is not going to be greatly helped by words. The presenter can do very little more than give us its title and tell us who is playing and/or singing it and, if it is recorded, which company has issued the recording. Playing our own music on a CD or iPod seems a far more inviting option. First, all of the identifying material will exist in the stable medium of print and thus allow us to peruse and re-peruse it at our leisure. Second, the music will only be that which we wish to hear: we won't have to listen to tracks we dislike or tracks that are played in a sequence that has been determined by someone else. Why, then, do we continue to listen to the radio?

It cannot simply be for the sound of the human voice, for as well as music we can obtain this from CDs and other recordings. It is evidently because of the need for human *co-presence*, to 'keep in touch' (Barnard, 2000, p. 105), an inherent feature of which is its juxtaposition with an unknown future. Whether or not I have already heard the voices on a recording, I know for a fact that they belong to the past: they are pre-ordained, cannot subsequently be modified, and are concluded. They are, in a word, dead – devoid of the spontaneity and uncertainty of outcome which characterise even aspects of theatrical performance. (Although it is usually scripted, no one performance will ever be exactly the same as another.) This explains why, when we desire 'company', we mean the company of living people and invariably turn not to CDs or DVDs but to radio and television. The phenomenon seems especially noticeable in local radio, where listeners feel the presenters are friends, and hail them as such if they meet them in the street. Moreover, it is company that we find entirely satisfying even when those whom we encounter in these media are not addressing us directly.

What all these examples – our literary passage, theatre and broadcast-ing – seem to reveal, then, is a desire for company *per se*. Each has its own particular purpose, whether to make an intellectual point, create an artistic experience or convey information, but prerequisite to it is the simple need to be in the presence of others, a need that communication analysts sometimes describe as *phatic*. It appears to characterise even a non-live medium like the cinema, for part of our pleasure in going to see a film is that others are in the auditorium with us. Despite our love of privacy, one that is frequently indulged by the way in which we consume radio, television and DVDs, we value liveness not just for the instantaneous nature of its messages but for the sense it gives us of being part of a larger community – all listening, or viewing and listen-ing, at the same time (Bourdon, 2000, p. 552). In other words, whether the primary medium is live (theatre, television, radio) or recorded (cinema and even the daily newspaper), a kind of live secondary communication – perhaps 'communion' or 'companionship' would be a better word – is established between the individual members of its audience, who are either co-present in time and space (theatre and cinema) or merely in time (television, radio, the daily newspaper): that is to say, in different places but all conscious of doing the same thing at that instant. (With the proliferation of channels and the growth of time-shift viewing, watching television has become much less of a communal activity than it used to be. Hence an emergence over the last ten or twelve years of shows like *Big Brother* (2000–) and *Strictly Come Dancing* (2004–), in which viewers can influence the outcome by phon-ing in their votes, would seem to be an attempt by broadcasters to bolster this dwindling sense of community. And perhaps it is not too fanciful to suggest that in the world of new media – a largely solitary and interactive one in which we perform things at times to suit ourselves – the growth of chat rooms, blogs and tweets, with their aim of prompting instant responses and spontaneous conversations, is the hankering for a liveness that is otherwise becoming hard to find. In our separate worlds, we want to know what others are doing at this moment, and that is often not very different from a craving for human contact.)

We have not discussed everything that is special about liveness, nor have we done full justice to the complexity of its relationship with recording, but since its other gratifications are better discussed in contexts where recording prevails – where sound reproduction and film are the norm – we will return to them later. Meanwhile, all these thoughts lead us to the big question. If liveness has so many desirable features, and if it is the quality that broadcasting possesses uniquely among the traditional mechanical media, why is so much of its content pre-recorded? Almost every kind of programming, including the news, contains at least some non-live material (Marriott, 2007, p. 48): indeed, it probably makes up a larger share of the total output than material that is live! But this is a question for another chapter.

4 Television and Recording (1): Replacing Liveness

The answer is an obvious if complex one which involves technological, economic, social and cultural factors; and like many an answer, it requites one question only to prompt another. We need to begin with a look at the technological development of recording, and for the most part, we will focus on television with just a glance or two at radio along the way, since radio forms the subject of another chapter.

What is recording? It is a way of defying the passage of time by capturing an event. The recording can then be played back in order to reflect the entire duration of the event, or it can be edited in order to suppress some parts of the event or to change its original sequence, or to do both of these things. In his study of sound media, Lars Nyre (2008, pp. 7–8) identifies three important features of recording which are equally applicable to the audiovisual media. First, it is a material commodity which is fixed in time. It has no continuity with the world. Second, recordings have their own space which is self-contained: we cannot enter it, but the sounds and images that inhabit it can be played back in all kinds of public and private places. Third, personality in recording is an elusive matter. There can be no direct contact between the person addressing the audience and the audience itself. Their relationship is asymmetrical and they are in their own separate and unbridgeable spaces.

Now let us look at television. As a live medium, television has no material carrier of its sounds and images in the way that traditional cinema has celluloid (Armes, 1988, p. 58). Images are scanned and sounds picked up, and both are transmitted to the viewer, who receives them almost instantaneously. When the British television service was launched by the BBC in 1936, it operated two systems of image scansion, one of them electronic and the other mechanical, and thanks to the superior definition of its images, the electronic system quickly prevailed. In theory, there was no reason why, among the images it scanned, television should not include those of cinema films, and it was in this respect that a powerful asset of the medium became relevant which was second only to its liveness: its *domesticity* (Crisell, 2006, p. 160). Despite making its debut in public places, television rapidly became a private, home-based medium. The public medium of cinema was hugely popular during the 1930s: indeed its audiences would not peak until 1946, when the annual number of picture-house admissions reached 1,635 million (Williams, 1998, p. 194). What could be more appealing than 'going to the cinema' in one's own home? Hence, although television was established as primarily a live medium, the screening of films occurred from its earliest years. Yet the process was attended with difficulties: ironically, the electronic system was at first not as successful in its scansion of film as the less light-sensitive mechanical system it rapidly displaced (Armes, 1988, p. 56). Moreover, the television image comprised twenty-five frames per second whereas cinema film's was twenty-four, the discrepancy appearing as a series of black bars on the TV screen (Winston, 1998, p. 268).

At first, there were no economic or cultural factors to force technological change. For the most part, the distributors of cinema films were unwilling to provide material to a medium that would steal audiences from their own and, as a monopoly serving only a handful of viewers, the television service had no incentive to pre-record its programmes. It broadcast only two hours of content per day and nothing at all on Sundays. Nevertheless, as the need grew stronger both for pre-recording programmes and for broadcasting material that had been pre-recorded by others, technological improvements kept pace with it. Radio had always been able to broadcast gramophone discs and, by the end of the 1930s, the pre-recording of its own programmes had become a relatively simple matter. By the middle of the 1950s, pre-recording would become similarly simple for television. But technological and social developments are inseparable from each other: technological innovation prompts social change, social change prompts technological innovation – and indeed such innovation is itself a form of social change. Thanks to the arrival of the 'utility' set in 1944, radio receivers had become relatively cheap by the end of the war (Pegg, 1983, p. 47–9) and television sets would become similarly affordable by the end of the 1950s.

The significance of this is that, by the 1960s, radios and televisions would exist in virtually every household in the country, and in many instances be individually owned. They were becoming ever more portable and were turned on and off at all hours of the day with little more sense of occasion than if they were the kitchen tap. This created a demand for an increase in both transmission hours and channels – hence for new or at least improved technologies not only to fuel the schedules but to increase the number of stations on the spectrum. In Britain, the BBC, at first a monopoly broadcaster and always supported in its public-service mission by the government, could mount a rearguard against this demand. Until 1972, television's transmission hours remained restricted. But competition, albeit limited and carefully regulated, had been introduced into British television back in 1955 and thenceforward there would be a proliferation of channels – at first hesitant, later rapid. (In radio, the proliferation would happen more steadily, thanks to the alleviation of spectrum scarcity through VHF/FM technology.)

The overall effect, then, was a burgeoning need for broadcast content, and the easiest way to meet it was through recording – the pre-recording of programmes or the use of commercial recordings in the form of cinema films for television and gramophone discs for radio. Across the Atlantic there was a further spur to the use of recording, a geographical problem from which Britain and most of Europe are free. North America is a vast continent with four main time zones (seven if one includes Newfoundland and Labrador in the east and Alaska in the west). In the early days of broadcasting, a network programme transmitted from New York at the prime time of 7.00 pm would be received in Los Angeles in mid-afternoon, when everyone was still at work. Before pre-recording arrived, the only solution to this problem was laborious and costly: to repeat the live programme at intervals throughout the day.

By the beginning of the 1950s, television had largely overcome its problems in screening recorded material, whether its own programmes or cinema films. Telerecording, the filming of live televised content from a monitor and known as 'kinescoping' in America, began in 1947 (Jacobs, 2000, p. 10) and, as the film distributors began to realise that there was money to be made from, as well as lost to, its great domesticated rival, there was a gradual easing of the restrictions on the televising of movies. In this, the American studios and distributors were more far-sighted than their British counterparts: after 1955, they made their libraries available to the television networks. Moreover, the contraction of the industry that had been caused by the rise of television had left them with surplus studio capacity. Mindful of the adage that 'if you can't beat them you should join them', Warner Bros. and a number of other companies did deals with the US TV networks to make film series exclusively for television (Turow, 1999, p. 237) and, by 1957, scores of these somewhat formulaic but highly successful series, mainly comedies, cop shows and Westerns, were beginning to be watched in both

American and British homes. Even that staid public-service broadcaster, the BBC, could not stand aloof from these developments: in 1957, it bought 100 old cinema movies from RKO and in 1959, another twenty-four from the Selznick Corporation (Briggs, 1995, p. 187).

With the arrival of video technology, the recording of television programmes took a giant leap forward, not least because it offered an instant-replay facility (Briggs, 1995, p. 834). In other respects, it was at first no better than telerecording, the poor-quality film made directly from TV monitors for subsequent re-broadcasting, but eventually it superseded the latter by offering the possibility of *pre*-recording programmes for live transmission (Cooke, 2003, p. 48; Marriott, 2007, p. 41). Video technology was American in origin: the Ampex system made its debut there in 1956. In Britain, the commercial company ATV was the first to acquire an Ampex machine and, in June 1958, to use it on air, but the BBC soon followed (Briggs, 1995, pp. 836–7). Not surprisingly, American television quickly adopted recording as the way to solve its time-zone problems. In 1957, more than 70 per cent of its prime-time transmissions were already non-live (Marriott, 2007, p. 41).

The consequences of television's ability to show pre-recorded material, whether cinematic or of its own making, have been enormous and interconnected. They are economic, social and aesthetic and we must now do our best to disentangle them. The most obvious consequence was an enormous expansion in the amount of material that television could broadcast. It could encompass the whole of an older genre, cinema – in theory at least, transmit its entire *oeuvre*. Moreover, it could pre-record any amount of material of its own. This meant that it could not only stockpile programmes for transmission at a later date, but *repeat* them. Repeats, especially of plays, had already been necessary in the era of virtually all-live broadcasting, something that could be seen as the micro-equivalent of a theatrical 'run', but they were hugely expensive to mount. One famous example is the 1954 television adaptation of George Orwell's novel *Nineteen Eighty-Four*, which was performed twice within a single week. However, *Nineteen Eighty-Four* was also a portent, for not only was it telerecorded but it contained fourteen pre-recorded inserts (Cooke, 2003, pp. 24–5).

It is worth stressing, then, that the pre-recording and stockpiling of material was not just strategically useful, it brought huge *economic* benefits. Performers and production staff no longer had to be reassembled or studios rebooked each time a particular play or other kind of programme was due to be transmitted. A much greater number of programmes could be made from the same resources, and repeated at almost no cost.

Recording, in a word, made possible what has been described as 'the economic development of the programme factory' (Bakewell and Garnham, 1970, p. 14). Neville Watson, the Chief Engineer of BBC Television, expressed it rather more graphically:

> Just one day in the studio and all the scenery is whipped out overnight, all the lights are re-set overnight and the next day a whole new production goes into the studio. ... This is where the economy is – not in the use of the apparatus, not in the number of technical staff that you use, but in the amount of production that you get out of a given set of facilities.
>
> (Bakewell and Garnham, 1970, pp. 21–2)

The developments in the technology of pre-recording caused a profound if subtle shift in what we might term the ideology of broadcasting, and particularly television, but in order to understand this we need to keep in mind the distinction between *recording* and *editing*. At first, telerecording and video recording achieved little more than their names imply: telerecording was used to copy programmes as they appeared on air for the purpose of re-broadcasting them, and video recordings were at first impossible to edit without damaging the tapes. Even when technicians could work out how to do it, the cost of each tape – £100 – was prohibitive (Cooke, 2003, p. 48). Hence, the primary purpose of both these kinds of recording was to capture whole programmes: they attempted almost nothing of the abridgement and/or resequencing that requires editing. This meant that until the late 1950s, recording underpinned rather than challenged the ideology of liveness in television.

Video technology is a vivid illustration of this. The tapes were at first so costly that they were regarded as more valuable than the programmes they carried, so they were routinely wiped and re-used (Jacobs, 2000, p. 11). But it seems to be the case that this was as much a reflection of ideology as of cost. Television was live and liveness deals in ephemerality, not permanence. Live material dissolves – perishes – and perishability is at once the source of its preciousness and its worthlessness. Since it is self-disposable, self-destructing, television's programmes should perish too. You no more retained them, except perhaps for *ad hoc* purposes such as the replacement of something that had to be cancelled or for a prompt re-broadcast to save the cost of a live repeat, than you retained yesterday's newspapers. (In fact, the ephemerality of newspapers is an aspect of what I shall be arguing shortly is a journalistic preoccupation with liveness that pre-dates broadcasting's and which is also evident in the regular and continual character of journalistic coverage.)

In the field of television drama, the pressure to record and retain rather than destroy programmes was on the face of it stronger. First, drama is less time sensitive than factual forms of programming: as Jérôme Bourdon (2000, p. 536) points out, liveness is of no value to fiction. Second, and related to this 'timelessness', drama has pretensions to artistic merit and thus makes us wish to preserve it. But here the ideology of liveness was reinforced not by what television shared with journalism but by what, in contrast, it shared with the traditional theatre.

In the beginning, television drama resembled certain other kinds of programme in being aesthetically unsure of itself. Was it merely a relay facility for live theatre or capable of producing its own forms of drama? Or was it some kind of rival to the cinema (Caughie, 1991, pp. 28–30)? For what were primarily technological reasons, drama on British television was probably typical of others countries' television drama in bearing a much closer resemblance to theatre than to cinema (Caughie, 2000, pp. 42–3). Its technique was to point a single camera at a theatrical set in order to create what has been termed 'the photographed stage play'. From 1947, telerecording provided the beginnings of a way in which television drama could overcome its rootedness in the theatre but, even as this happened, the ideology of liveness was fighting a rearguard action. TV drama, it was felt, should be live not only because television itself is live – what in the light of our recent comparison we might perceive as the 'journalistic' case for liveness – but because the traditional theatre was live. Hence, the more cinematic the drama became, the more it sought to proclaim its affinity with the theatre (Auslander, 1999, p. 22).

In Britain, this tendency was reinforced by the philosophy of public service, which, as embodied in the BBC monopoly, attached a primary importance to the edifying role of broadcasting. For public-service purposes, the BBC aspired to the cultural status of the theatre, not the cinema. It is true that it occasionally showed cinema films, but these were seen as extraneous to television's own repertoire, the contents of a different medium which it deigned to relay merely in order to fill gaps in its schedules. Cinema was widely thought of as low-brow, partly because it was relatively new-fangled and partly because in being able to be more spectacular than the conventional theatre, it was less verbal – less 'literary'. On this view, television was a transparent medium that existed simply to relay the theatrical canon, the conventional and hallowed plays of Shakespeare, Ibsen, Shaw and the like (Cooke, 2003,

p. 10). That the view was widely held is attested by the fact that the BBC could often get the *stage* rights for the television transmission of a play but not the *mechanical* rights (Jacobs, 2000, p. 12).

What was integral to this traditional understanding of drama, then, was its ephemerality: if the performance of a theatrical play lasted only an hour or two and then disappeared for ever, the same should be true of a televised play. This raises the interesting question of how, historically speaking, an evanescent art form like the theatre should have been able to acquire such high cultural status. The answer would seem to be that this status rests largely on that part of the theatrical performance which is permanent, namely the script. We think of drama as essentially a *literary* art form, its status attaching to the playwrights rather than the actors because until recently the performances of the latter could never be captured (Crisell, 2006, p. 6).

In any event, British television's allegiance to the traditional theatre meant that, during its first years, it offered only adaptations of theatrical plays: it did not presume to create plays of its own. Even in the era of recording, the old ideology of liveness died hard. In America, the shooting of TV drama on film began early in order to solve the problem of transmitting to different time zones (Cooke, 2003, pp. 22–3), but this was not so in Britain. Of the twenty-three plays that comprised the first season of the BBC's *Play for Today* (1970), only six (26 per cent) were shot on film, and of the twenty-seven plays of its last season (1979–80) only fifteen (55 per cent) were filmed (Cooke, 2003, p. 92). Even dramas that were filmed were not necessarily retained: between 1955 and 1976, the hugely popular police series *Dixon of Dock Green* ran to 430 episodes, yet only thirty survive (Cooke, 2003, p. 50).

What no doubt helped to maintain the ideology of liveness was the fact that the picture quality of recorded content was clearly inferior to that of live transmission, something which caused a particular problem when recorded sequences were inserted into live programmes. The viewer then encountered what looked like ontological jump-cuts: an action unfolding as if in the continuous present would contain sequences that clearly belonged in a different time. Gradually, however, it became harder to tell from appearances what was live and what was not. As the recording media improved in quality and became cheaper and thus more readily editable, the ideology of liveness, whether journalistic or theatrical, became overlaid by another ideology – of television as a locus of creativity, a source of works of art whether factual or fictional. Pre-recording allowed elements of programmes to be shot repeatedly until they were perfect. From a number of 'takes' the optimum performance of both presenters and performers could be selected, if necessary as a composite of all of them; mistakes and technical glitches could be eliminated; redundancies and hiatuses could be removed, notably those that often occurred in outside broadcasts where events were not under the control of television itself: and finally the programmes could, if required, be re-ordered into sequences that were more logical or aesthetically pleasing. What lent urgency to these improvements were soaring audiences and quickening competition: if a programme looked badly made or contained stretches when the viewers were waiting for something to happen, there was a growing risk that they would switch to another channel.

Broadcasters came to realise (as, when off-air home recording arrived some twenty years later, audiences would) that the preservable nature of programmes was, like that of film, a way of enhancing their artistic impact and value. If a programme no longer vanished irretrievably into thin air, if you could view or hear it more than once, you had a better chance of appreciating its merits. In the field of drama, the single tele-vision play grew aesthetically closer to the cinema by incorporating location filming and showing the effects of editing. Scenes typically became shorter and were characterised by a greater sense of mobility, and there was a reduction in the importance, or at least prominence, of dialogue and a commensurate growth of visual interest.

The enhanced artistic status not just of drama but other kinds of pro-gramme had an important consequence: it turned them into *commodities*, things that could be bought and sold among broadcasters (Caughie, 1991, p. 39; Caughie, 2000, p. 54; Jacobs, 2000, pp. 12–13). It might be considerably cheaper for a television network to buy certain programmes than to make them: on the other hand, some programme-makers might not be broadcasters at all. This change in the artistic and economic status of individual programmes seems to be reflected in the semantic history of the word itself. At first, the very notion of 'a programme' in the sense of a separate broadcast item was uncertain: the first radio stations transmitted a live stream of content – readings, recitations, sketches, songs and other musical pieces – within which the distinctions and boundaries were not always clear. Hence the original meaning of *programme* was, in the words of the *Shorter Oxford English Dictionary*, 'A radio service or station providing a regular succession of programmes [*sic*] on a particular frequency'. In other words, the term was largely synonymous with what we would now describe as a *channel* or *network*: the BBC operated the Light Programme, the Forces' Programme, the Third Programme and so on.

Gradually, however, the more modern sense came to the fore: 'A broadcast presentation treated as a single item for scheduling purposes, being broadcast between stated times and without interruption, except perhaps for news bulletins or advertisements'. It is probably no accident that this second meaning of 'programme', something that is offered as a self-contained artefact within a channel or network, began to dominate at just that period – from the late 1940s to the early 1960s – that a substantial amount of material on radio and television was being pre-recorded. Moreover, the repeated airings that recording encouraged took place not just on a channel or channels operated by a single broadcaster but on channels run by a number of broadcasters, many of them located in different parts of the world. For instance, a huge traffic in television programmes developed within the anglophone countries which, with the help of dubbing or subtitles, was rapidly extended to those which spoke other languages (Hesmondhalgh, 2002; Flew, 2007).

However, pre-recording prompted another phenomenon which greatly increased the marketability of programmes and which perhaps constitutes broadcasting's greatest cultural achievement: the growth of *seriality*. Seriality is, in fact, a more widespread phenomenon than we might recognise, and some sense of this will be helpful before we focus on those manifestations of it that are of relevance to our study. It is not simply that the great majority of television and radio programmes are part of a series: we could argue that the whole of broadcasting embodies the principle of seriality, a characteristic it shares with print journalism. Newspapers are consumed day by day, periodicals week by week or month by month – as instalments – and indeed many news stories are serial in character, unfolding over days, weeks or longer. We might therefore stretch a point and see the seriality of journalism, especially newspaper journalism, as the aspiration to a liveness it can never actually attain. The aim is that readers are 'kept abreast' of events. These are covered by the newspapers as they happen, and the reader not only learns about them within a very short time but will learn tomorrow how they have developed. Just as ephemerality is an aspect of the live world, so it is also a characteristic of journalism. When today becomes yesterday, the newspaper is discarded and replaced by another one. This is the next best thing to liveness: coverage that is, if not *continuous*, at least *continual*.

So what of the serial character of broadcasting? There is nothing in theory to say that broadcasting has to be serial. It does not have to aspire to liveness because it *is* live, so it could transmit material in a sporadic rather than regular way. Nevertheless, to be truly significant, the feat of liveness has to be frequently repeated, for liveness is constantly dissolving: the present slides into the past. Moreover, and as we have already seen, since television and radio sets were located in the home and in growing numbers individually owned, the ease with which they could be accessed produced a demand for daily transmissions, lengthening transmission hours, eventually transmissions round the clock. Since broadcasting is live, its coverage of events by way of rolling news channels can indeed be continuous and not just continual: such channels have now been with us for more than twenty years. This is the kind of liveness which print journalism can only envy, an illustration of what we might term 'hyper-seriality'. Nevertheless, even if there are compelling reasons for *broadcasting* to be serial, its *programmes* do not have to be. They could be one-offs and sometimes are and, in the early days of broadcasting, such programmes were common. Our interest here is in the seriality of particular kinds of content.

We need to be clear that seriality did not begin with the availability of pre-recording: in the era of virtually all-live broadcasting, there were many series and some serials. Nor is serial content peculiar to broadcasting. During the nineteenth century, novels were serialised in magazines, partly as a way of filling column space over a number of issues, partly as a way of spreading publication costs for both the publishers of the novels and their readers, and partly as a way of securing the readers' loyalty to both the magazines and the novels. Dickens, Thackeray, Trollope and George Eliot were among the authors who benefited from serialisation. Series and serials were also an early feature of the cinema: they appeared in the UK and France in 1912 and in the US in 1914 (Manvell, 1972, p. 50), and were plainly intended to ensure repeat business at the picture-houses. But in broadcasting, the demand for content that was created by the domesticity and individuality of its consumption was unprecedented. The most efficient way of meeting it was seriality, and the most efficient means of creating serial content was pre-recording. Let us look at it a little more closely.

To use a given set of studio facilities to pre-record and stockpile an assortment of programmes was certainly less expensive than broadcasting each of them as live events, but it was hardly cheap: and whether as live productions or pre-recordings, single plays have always been especially costly. Moreover, single programmes are difficult to sell to other broadcasters: they are of limited duration and hard to fit into schedules in a way that will attract audiences. Pre-recording became significantly cheaper only if the programmes that were stockpiled were all of a kind or in some way linked to one another. In an increasingly competitive environment, it kept down costs because in a single production sequence and from a single set of resources both human and material, several programmes could be made for not very much more than the price of one. Indeed, one could see the series or serial not as several thematically linked programmes but as a single gigantic programme which is divided into segments that are then transmitted at intervals. Moreover, unlike the conventional single programme, the series or serial is highly marketable. It can be sold to other broadcasters as a package, a way of filling air-time and building the loyalty of audiences over a period of weeks, months or even longer. We can say that by adopting the techniques of mass production, pre-recorded seriality marked the point at which broadcasting became fully industrialised.

In the following discussion, we will focus on serial forms of broadcast drama because they represent television's and radio's highest endeavours as creative media, but we must remember that seriality characterises much, probably most, broadcast output and therefore that some of what we say about drama will be applicable to other kinds of programming. What the discussion illustrates above all is the way in which new kinds of audience demand combine with new technologies to generate new art forms (Crisell, 2006, pp. 114–17).

Serial drama takes one of two forms: the *series* – a collection of separate, self-contained episodes that focus on a single character, theme or situation and can be broadcast and consumed in any order; and *serials* proper – episodes that are sequentially linked and are therefore broadcast, and ideally consumed, in a particular order. In recent years there has been something of a tendency to blur the two forms. A drama that is for the most part a series may include episodes that presuppose the audience's knowledge of something that has happened in an earlier episode: it may consist of self-contained stories but within an overall narrative progression. Nevertheless the distinction between the two is still broadly tenable.

How, then, does serial drama in either form differ from its theatrical and cinematic predecessors? First, and obviously, it is much longer – sometimes infinitely so. The famous radio serial *The Archers* has so far lasted for sixty years and shows no sign of reaching a conclusion! Even a serial of six thirty-minute episodes, short by broadcast standards, would be twice the length of the average cinema feature film and a third longer than the average stage play. It pushes broadcast drama nearer to the classic (often epic) novel, a genre that it likes to adapt, than to the cinema. Second, those serials and series that are written for broadcast, as distinct from being adapted for it, often lack 'closure', the neat narrative conclusion that typifies traditional drama. A third feature of the serial is the regular use of a 'cliff-hanger', a suspenseful moment at the end of each episode whose obvious purpose is to ensure that the audience watch or listen to the next one.

The form of broadcast serial drama known as soap opera has certain other distinctive features. First, it carries multiple plotlines, some of which develop and some of which do not: there is no single narrative perspective on the action. Second, there is a large cast of characters, including a range of protagonists: given the lack of a single narrative point of view, there is also no single hero on whom the action is focused. Third, soap operas are mostly dramas of a particular domestic and daily kind and their pace is slow. The stories and their settings – a family, a street, a small community, a workplace – are more mundane, less exotic, than is the case in many conventional dramas. Fourth, the treatment of time is less elliptical than in many traditional stories. In the latter, those periods of time in which nothing happens that contributes to their development are simply skipped over, but in soap operas the action develops more or less contemporaneously with real time: a week in the life of the characters is a week in the life of the viewers and listeners. Even if for a week or two certain of the characters do not form the focus of attention, we have the firm impression that they are getting on with their lives, as it were, elsewhere.

The distinctive features of serial drama, as indeed of seriality in general, are of course attributable to the unprecedented circumstances and requirements of the audience and at this point, it might be helpful to remind ourselves of them. If things can be live in broadcasting they should be because, historically at least, liveness is broadcasting's unique advantage: this is what audiences want from it. Hence much pre-recording is in the service of liveness and will as far as possible pretend to be live. Yet watching television or listening to the radio is not like the experience of the theatre, cinema, concert hall or sports stadium. We don't have to leave the comfort of our own space and we don't have to pay an admission fee: there is little sense of occasion. We watch and listen each and every day – as often as not when we have nothing better to do, or as an accompaniment to (usually humdrum) chores. All of this creates a demand for a volume and variety of content that cannot possibly be satisfied by liveness alone. Hence soap operas can be seen as an example *par excellence* of the challenges broadcasting faces and the way it seeks to meet them: they reflect its need to pre-record material on the one hand and to affirm its liveness on the other; yet since, given the scale of the demand for material, liveness is impossible, live-seemingness is the next best thing. This is why so many soaps are mundane, unending and, as far as possible, avoid ellipsis in their representation of time: life is like that.

Soap operas thus stand in a different relation to the world from most other sorts of drama. We noted earlier that liveness is of no value to fiction, and therefore that drama, a form of fiction, does not *have* to be live, a fact that is demonstrated by cinema. Yet we are also aware that drama is historically live since it has its origins in the theatre. So what sort of liveness, or seeming liveness, do we mean here? Traditional theatre is live in the sense that the audience witnesses the performance at the instant it occurs. But such liveness pertains *only* to the performance, not to the world that is being depicted. In a live performance of Shakespeare's *Hamlet* the world of Elsinore is not contemporaneous with our own, as the language and costumes of its characters amply illustrate. In most soap operas, however, not only do the performance and consumption seem to occur at the same instant: there appears to be no 'performance' at all in the sense that the world they depict seems entirely contemporaneous with our own. When this illusion is threatened – when, for example, some outdoor scenes reveal trees in full leaf that are now bare or the snow on the ground that melted last week – it can come as a shock. Indeed the producers of soap operas will go to considerable lengths to bolster the sense of up-to-dateness. If, between the pre-recording and transmission of a particular episode, a major real-world event has occurred that the characters would be likely to refer to, the actors are often recalled to the studio to record fresh dialogue. Hence, in its live-seeming, serial attempts to convey a world that is contiguous with our own, soap opera perhaps owes as much to journalism as to the conventional theatre. It is a form of (almost invariably) pre-recorded drama that nevertheless brings to the genre the ideology, if not the actuality, of liveness.

Let me try to sum up the argument I have been making. The number and scale of radio and television serials are made possible only by pre-recording, yet many serials, and pretty much all soap operas, also seek to preserve broadcasting's aura of liveness by portraying a world that seems to be in a temporal and spatial continuum with our own. We can also say that broadcast drama starts out as *theatrical* but thanks to recording technology becomes *cinematic*; and finally, thanks both to recording technology and the situation and demands of its audience, adopts seriality and so becomes both *telegenic* and *radiogenic*.

Serial drama is, however, only one manifestation of the seriality inherent in many – most – forms of radio and television content, and this seriality is very largely the consequence of the practice of pre-recording. Since the 1960s, when pre-recording became cheaper and easier, liveness has become increasingly confined to particular genres and niches, to programmes that are unique or whose regularity is infrequent or whose outcome cannot be foreknown: the news, ceremonial occasions, sporting fixtures, catastrophes, one-off spectaculars and more recently, certain kinds of reality TV. But even programmes which are promoted as live, and for the most part are, often contain pre-recorded elements (Marriott, 2007, pp. 41–2). On the other hand, pre-recording prevails in all those programmes that are less time sensitive: drama, light entertainment and certain factual forms such as features and documentaries that deal in the more enduring, less 'eventful' aspects of contemporary life.

As was mentioned earlier, the picture quality of pre-recorded content was once noticeably inferior to that of live transmissions and seemed especially incongruous when it was dropped into live plays. Eventually, however, it became impossible to see a difference between live and pre-recorded images, and the only way of inferring it was from the kind of extraneous knowledge about leaves and snow that I referred to just now, or from references in the accompanying commentary or dialogue. It is just possible that, because of the growth of newer media that are live or nearly live, the liveness of broadcasting is not as significant as it was. In any event, it is reasonable to assume that most broadcast material is now pre-recorded: there are some radio and television channels which carry no live material at all. Yet in much broadcasting there is still a pretence of liveness, even in programmes that could not possibly be live (Ellis, 2002, pp. 34–5).

We are therefore confronted by a further question. Liveness may be broadcasting's unique advantage, historically at least, and the characteristic that audiences want from it. But the fact remains that, due to a number of wholly respectable economic, social and cultural reasons, much of the liveness, whether of soaps or many other kinds of programme, is a sham – and one that the audiences can generally see through. Why, then, do broadcasters maintain it and viewers and listeners continue to acquiesce in it? The answer to this question must wait for a later chapter.

5 Radio and Recording: Mostly Music

Many of the advantages of recording which we have outlined in relation to television apply also to radio. It enables sound broadcasters to stockpile and trade programmes and to fill air-time through the more efficient creation of serial content. Yet radio is worth a separate look partly because its history is slightly different and partly because one of its programming staples is music, and the relationship between liveness and recording in music poses some intriguing questions. These are not only about music – notably, What constitutes musicianship? – but about radio: What kind of medium is it and what does it exist to do?

Radio's history is different in the sense that there was never any technical difficulty about incorporating pre-recorded sound into its output in the way that television had a difficulty with the pre-recorded images of cinema. But as the older of the two media, radio had to face questions about the nature and purposes of broadcasting that had been at least partly resolved by the time television arrived. Did it exist to diffuse live material alone, or recordings too? And if the latter, should these be only the recordings that the broadcasters themselves had made or should they extend to commercial recordings, such as gramophone discs? We will consider these questions first in relation to general programmes and then to radio's extensive musical output.

In the BBC, there existed from the beginning an almost moral feeling that the proper business of broadcasting was to provide live material (Chignell, 2009, p. 46), and this feeling was probably shared by many early broadcasters. But, as with television, practical necessity soon overrode loftier matters of principle. In the US, for instance, there was the problem of transmitting live programmes across time zones, while in Britain a difficulty arose for two commercial stations, Radios Normandy and Luxembourg, which aimed to compete with the BBC. Since the latter had been granted a domestic monopoly by the government, they were obliged to beam their programmes from the European mainland. But the performers whom they engaged were for the most part based in Britain and not always able or willing to travel to Europe.

The solution was to record the programmes in London – a task which was undertaken by J. Walter Thompson and other big advertising agencies (Street, 2002, p. 41) – and then fly the recordings out to the stations for transmission back to Britain.

Yet the overwhelming challenge to all-live output was undoubtedly the fact of a mainly home-based audience whose consumption of radio was at once casual and greedy. Indeed, because the audience would listen to the radio while engaged in a variety of activities and not merely when at leisure, the demand for its content until fairly recently exceeded the demand for television's. (What has changed is that people are now much more blasé about television and use it in the same secondary way that they use radio, even though their primary activity may preclude them from watching it for more than brief spells: and to meet this fitful viewing, TV's transmission hours have expanded accordingly.)

At first consisting of aluminium discs which could capture only fifteen minutes of sound, recording technology developed steadily, if in different forms, throughout the 1930s, and in 1934, the BBC was already able to set up its Recorded Programmes Library (Chignell, 2009, p. 44; Street, 2002, p. 49; Parker, 1977, p. 64). In the same year, portable sound-recording machines began to be used for the gathering of actuality, especially for inclusion in news programmes and for documentaries the BBC hired a recording van from a film company (Scannell, 1986, p. 12). Not surprisingly, the practice of pre-recording programmes was given a huge boost by the exigencies of the Second World War (1939–45). First, it often removed the need to bring broadcasters into studios which were at risk of aerial bombardment. Second, if the studios were bombed and live broadcasts disrupted, it was a source of reserve material. Third, it enabled the BBC to more easily obtain the clearance of 'sensitive' material which it was obliged to submit in advance to the Ministry of Information. But what were also of great value to the BBC were the recordings of programmes that were made by overseas broadcasters. At a time when domestic material was often in short supply, it imported shows from the American networks and introduced British listeners to such stars as Bob Hope, Bing Crosby, Glenn Miller and Jack Benny (Crisell, 2002, pp. 61–2, 65).

Every bit as important was the use of recording in the production of news. Listeners not only craved information about the progress of the conflict but the actuality that would illustrate it, and since most of this came from the battle zones, the BBC's engineers created for its war reporters a 'midget' portable sound recorder that weighed twenty kilos and was issued with twelve double-sided discs (Briggs, 1970, pp. 654–8).

The material they gathered was not only inserted into the news bulletins but formed the basis of the programme *War Report*, which began in 1944 and won vast audiences.

In the post-war decades sound-recording technology became better, cheaper and more flexible and, as it did so, the amount of pre-recorded content on the radio steadily increased just as it did on television – and for much the same economic and strategic reasons. Asa Briggs (1995, p. 833) has claimed that in 1960 about half of all the BBC's radio programmes were broadcast live but that by the mid-1970s hardly any were. One interesting blend of the live and the recorded is radio news. For obvious reasons it must always be presented live, yet the actuality that 'brings it alive' is almost invariably pre-recorded: hence the assertion that the news emphasises the liveness of radio (Chignell, 2009, p. 165) is a somewhat paradoxical one. However, certain topical content such as sports commentary remains almost wholly live, and features and discussion programmes will often seek to affirm their liveness by including a phone-in that enables listeners to question and argue with the studio participants (Chignell, 2009, p. 89).

The relationship between radio and music, whether live or recorded, is a fascinating one. At the beginning of regular broadcasting (1922 in Britain), there was undoubtedly a general assumption that the medium would originate its own musical content rather than simply air gramophone records. The latter were already a popular mass medium which was diffused through its own retail outlets. But as in the case of radio's non-musical content, practical considerations soon prevailed, chief among them the simple need to fill air-time. Nevertheless, records were mostly seen as understudies to live musical performance, a fact that explains why Phonographic Performance Limited, the agency which collected royalties on behalf of the record companies and in league with the Musicians' Union, was able to drive such a hard bargain with the BBC over 'needle-time' – the number of commercially produced records that the latter would be allowed to play on air (Barnard, 1989, p. 27).

The BBC had been broadcasting for five years before it launched a record show. Rather stiffly entitled a 'Gramophone Record Recital', it was presented by Christopher Stone and offered a cheerfully eclectic mix of music that embraced both Mendelssohn and Fats Waller (Gifford, 1985, p. 276). Until well into the 1970s, live music was commonly heard on British radio, but what acted as a broker to the perfect marriage of radio and records was the rise of television. From the second half of the 1950s, radio's problem was that television not only stole most of its audience but threatened its repertoire of programmes: there was no longer a demand for the range of content it had hitherto offered because those elements of it that could profit from a visual dimension were now being broadcast on television. Nevertheless, as a non-visual and mostly secondary medium, radio was still wanted for news, mostly in summary form and above all, for music. But why did it meet this demand with records and not with live music?

In its public-service role, the BBC still broadcasts some live music on its radio networks. But for commercial radio, especially that which was not bound by the stricter tenets of public service, to broadcast music recordings made much more sense, both economically and artistically. First, records enabled stations to offer a much greater variety of sound than could be made by a single musician or group of musicians. Second, live musicians are costly, a large number of them may be difficult to assemble within a space that is suitable for broadcasting and after playing for long spells, they become tired. Third, there is a risk that live musicians will make mistakes, whereas thanks to multiple 'takes', editing and other technical enhancements, a recording represents the best performance of which they are capable – indeed something *better* than their best performance since it can be a synthesis of *several* performances.

Finally, there is an argument for playing records on the radio that goes to the very heart of the difference between the public-service and commercial philosophies of broadcasting because it addresses the question, What is the medium for? As we have seen, the early belief among broadcasters was that radio should carry only such material as is unobtainable by commercial means, and this was essentially a *public-service* belief because it implies a view of broadcasting as a unique resource, a way of providing what other media do not provide, or do not provide as accessibly. The newer belief was that records on the radio could serve not just as a stop-gap, a cheap and easy way to fill air-time, but as a sales pitch to listeners: if they liked what they heard, they could then buy them from a retail outlet and play them whenever they chose. From this perspective, the whole concept of music radio, by which we mean the almost continuous transmission of recorded music, is a *commercial* one, for the records act as a series of adverts – exhortations to the listener to buy them. It is therefore arguable that when the BBC launched Radio 1 in 1967, a network which aspired to play almost continuous recorded music even if needle-time restrictions at first prevented this, its public-service values had been compromised by a commercial ethic. For the first time in its history, it was running a network that did not provide a miscellany of material that might be interesting or valuable *per se* and which was difficult to access by other means, but a network that transmitted streamed content for the promotion of products (Crisell, 1994, p. 73).

The philosophical difference between public service and commercialism in broadcasting, and – at least in respect of its recorded-music networks – the BBC's shift from the former to the latter, are worth emphasising, because the launch of Radio 1 is often represented as nothing more than a pragmatic response to the pirate, all-music stations that had challenged the corporation's monopoly. However, I would wish to argue that the old public-service view is not just some cosily edifying theory that was imposed on broadcasting without much concern for what it is or can do but was based on a much clearer sense of its unique character and potential than the commercial view. To make this argument, I need to look a little more closely at the relationship that exists between liveness and recording in music.

So far, liveness has been our yardstick: that is to say, we have considered recordings largely in terms of liveness – as a substitute for it, an imitation of it, an ancillary to it. In its infancy, the aim of recording was simply to reproduce the original live sound as faithfully as possible, and so it fitted in well with the pristine aims of broadcasting. If, for whatever reason, a musical performance could not be live, at least it could be listened to *as if it were*. Some recordings were commercial – that is to say, intended for sale to the general public – but others were single items or existed in very limited numbers and were intended primarily for use by broadcasters: only after transmission might they be copied in sufficient numbers for sale to the public. However, from about the mid-1950s and for two main reasons, the character and purposes of commercial music recording changed radically. First, records and record players became more widely affordable and of better quality: more people wished to buy and play records than ever before (Crisell, 2002, p. 141). Second, and quite suddenly, a new kind of popular music called rock-and-roll mushroomed into a massive and prolonged craze on both sides of the Atlantic.

Rock-and-roll illustrated that technology was changing the way music was being performed and recorded as well as the equipment on which its recordings were being played. Despite its simple and largely rural origins in black rhythm-and-blues and white country-and-western music, rock was 'electric' not just figuratively but literally, for its key instrument, the guitar, was electrically amplified and its sound electronically treated through tremolo units, fuzz-boxes, echo-chambers and the like. Indeed apart from drums, the classic rock line-up consisted *only* of electric guitars: lead guitar, rhythm guitar and bass guitar. Among other things technology is labour-saving, and I have suggested elsewhere that this is as true of the performance of rock music as of other technologised activities (Crisell, 2002, p. 103). A rock band of four or six musicians can make a sound that is as loud as, even louder than, that of a full orchestra playing traditional instruments – and with much less physical effort. Even the traditional instruments it sometimes incorporates, such as piano, saxophone and drums, are frequently amplified, but the essence and innovation of rock music was the electric guitar: to this day it is the icon of the genre.

Yet new technology not only determined how rock and 'pop', the broader kind of music into which rock partly mutated, would be performed: it also shaped the way in which it was recorded. In essence certain elements of the music were created not by musicians but by technicians, for the music originated not in theatres, ballrooms and concert halls but in sound laboratories, better known as 'studios'. As Roy Armes (1988, p. 81) put it, rock 'became the first form of popular music for which the record is the key element – the "original" as it were': and this was because the primary aim was not to recapture or promote live performances but, much more profitably, to sell records. Moreover, recording was less and less a matter of simply capturing a tune that the musicians performed in the studio in the way that they might perform it in a concert hall, and more and more of blending several studio performances to which extra sounds, some of them electronically generated, would be added. The result, then, was not so much a true reproduction of what the musicians had played, or were capable of playing, as a kind of layered patchwork made up of sounds assembled from a number of 'takes', sounds multitracked and superimposed, sounds sampled, edited, mixed and repeated, and often enhanced by pieces of equipment that were neither wholly musical instruments nor simply machines: keyboards, synthesizers, drum pads. We might describe this as *industrial* music, factory music – like most factory products something that is created in huge numbers, each unit the clone of every other, for the purpose of selling to a mass public.

Quoting Roy Armes, I have just described the record as the 'original' of rock music but it might be truer to say that there is no original at all. There is no single, continuous and complete performance from which the recordings have been made, for even the master disc or tape or sound file which is their source is an amalgam: it is not the capture of a musical event that occurred in the real world. Let me try to summarise. Traditional music, by which I mean any kind of music – classical, jazz, folk, popular – that pre-dated the birth of electronic rock and pop music, habitually existed in live performances that recordings sought to capture. These could be multiply copied for commercial purposes or used for single broadcasts, but in a sense the uses to which they were put were secondary to the task of capture. The recording of rock and pop music, however, was as much a matter of *creation* as capture: songs were constructed piecemeal in the studio, usually before any public performance of them, and with the primary aim of replication and selling. And the consequence is that rock and pop have inverted the previous relationship between live performance and recording. In traditional music, the challenge was for the recording to capture the live performance: *the recording aspired to the live.* In rock and pop, the challenge very swiftly became to reproduce in live performance the sound that had been manufactured in the studio (Auslander, 1999, p. 31): *the live aspired to the recording.* Yet precisely because the studio sound was created with the help of elaborate technology, this was – and is – quite hard to achieve.

Since rock and pop music had its origins mainly in recording, needle-time restrictions on music stations like Radio 1 flew in the face of what we might term historical inevitability. Quite aside from the fears of the Musicians' Union that the playing of records would make live performance largely redundant, the restrictions stemmed from the mistaken belief that studio technology was a mere enhancement of the music rather than something integral to it. Hence, and as the disc jockey Tony Blackburn (2007, p. 24) amusingly recounts, in the early years of Radio 1, listeners might hear the Northern Dance Orchestra doing live versions of the Rolling Stones' 'Jumping Jack Flash' or Jimi Hendrix's 'Purple Haze'. Played with instruments which belonged to a quite different musical idiom, they were comically inept – unintended parodies. BBC Television was cannier. In order to promote their records, singers and bands flocked to appear on its hugely popular programme, *Top of the Pops* (1964–2006), but they did not perform their music: they mimed to it.

For this reason, traditional musicians have often despised rock and pop artists, regarding them as incapable of producing a decent sound without the help of a great deal of technology, but we need to understand how far such a view is justifiable. We should begin by noting that any music which involves an instrument, even a penny-whistle or a tin drum, is technologised. A traditional orchestra with its panoply of instruments, not one of them powered by electricity, is nonetheless every bit as dependent on its forms of mediation as a rock group. So whence springs the sense of difference?

Electricity does seem to be the point at issue, because it is not only labour-saving but skill-saving: the effect of all the electronic mediation is to weaken the connection between the physical effort and virtuosity of the performers on the one hand and the finished sound on the other. Since the primary habitat of rock and pop music is the recording studio, some of the traditional attributes of musicianship have been ceded to technology. (Another way to view this phenomenon is to *extend* the idea of musicianship to embrace technical virtuosity, but this is seldom done, and it remains true that, with such notable exceptions as Mike Oldfield, Kraftwerk and Harold Faltermeyer, musicians and technicians tend to remain in separate categories.)

Rock and pop artists are not wholly insensitive to the charge of limited musicianship and respond to it in two main ways. The first is to attempt to produce as good a sound in concert as they create in the studio and on record, one which either simulates the manufactured sound or is of an equivalent quality to it. Philip Auslander (1999, p. 26) has shrewdly observed that it is only within an 'economy of repetition' – by which he means, among other things, the mass production of music records – that liveness assumes significance. Hence, as long ago as 1965, the Rolling Stones produced an EP ('extended play' record) defiantly titled *Got Live If You Want It!*, a selection of their concert performances perhaps intended to dispel the belief that they did not play their own music in the studio. (So closely intertwined have liveness and recording become that we might barely notice the irony of a *record* proclaiming its *liveness*! Evidently the aim of the EP was not only to be as good as a conventional record but to offer, either in the music itself or in the audience's reactions to it, a raw, impromptu quality that most records lack.)

Yet even the live performances of rock bands will not assuage the cynicism of every old-fashioned musician. At a concert of traditional music, the orchestra arrives, its members unpack their instruments and spend a few moments tuning them, and then it is ready to play. At a rock concert, the preparations seem almost comically unwieldy: the audience cannot fail to be struck by the thickets of microphones for both singers and instruments, the spaghetti of cables, cliffs of amplifiers, vast mixing console sometimes suspended above the auditorium – and, not least, the endless sound checks before the bands are ready to perform. Hence, the second way in which rock and pop artists might seek to affirm their musicianship is to perform 'unplugged', using acoustic instruments without technological enhancement. Their aim is self-evidently not to replicate or emulate the sound of their records but to do different versions of them, or indeed to perform material that they have not hitherto recorded. Yet even unplugged performances are not devoid of technological mediation, for the voices and instruments are always amplified.

So where does all this leave radio? If the music in the overwhelming majority of its music shows is pre-recorded, what is the point of playing it on a live medium? As we noted in Chapter 3, the music is nevertheless framed within a live broadcast. A presenter or disc-jockey satisfies our need for human co-presence, as indeed does our awareness when we are listening that countless others are listening at the same time (Chignell, 2009, p. 33). We conceded that playing our own records is often preferable to listening to the radio since they exactly mirror our tastes and mean that we never have to listen to anything we dislike. Yet resigning our choice to another can also be pleasurable because it allows us to experience the delights of novelty and serendipity. Moreover, even though the playlist has probably not been compiled by the presenter, the records seem to be associated with his or her personality, which in a curious way remains central to the show. Records come and go but the shows are essentially judged in terms of, for example, Chris Moyles or Sara Cox on Radio 1 or Chris Evans or Ken Bruce on Radio 2.

The importance of the presenters is illustrated by the fact that they have been very largely retained, even though, thanks to station websites, webcasting and the presence of rolling text on digital receivers, their once primary need to identify the records has diminished. Yet the transmission of a lengthy sequence of records which is not punctuated by the voice of a presenter, something which is a feature of the off-peak times of the schedule on some radio stations, makes for rather bleak and unnerving listening. Since, however easily it can be pre-recorded, the human voice is indelibly associated with liveness, many commercial radio operators turn instead to 'robo-jock' shows, presented programmes which have nevertheless been prefabricated either for use during the 'graveyard' hours of the schedule or for transmission at different times on the different stations that they operate. To the listener the robo-jock shows are of course indistinguishable from live ones, but if their true nature were more widely known, it is conceivable that there might be a reaction against them.

Nevertheless, the fact remains that all these shows are *music* shows – that however much an individual presenter might influence the listeners' decision to tune in, the music is their primary reason for doing so, for if their desire is for continuous human company they can turn to an all-talk channel. Yet since the record manufacturers no longer need radio quite as much as they did – or to put it another way, customers can with increasing ease access their products by means other than the 'implicit' adverts of radio – it is perhaps time that the medium weaned itself from its reliance on recorded music.

Let us consider the matter by once again adopting an historical perspective. It is possible to see radio and television on the one hand and records on the other as forms of broadcasting, the diffusion of content to a large, dispersed and remote audience. By either atmospheric means or wires and cables, radio and television diffuse a series of single items to their audience. These items are live, or at least pre-recorded exclusively for their own purposes, or for sale to the public only after their diffusion through these media has taken place. Records are mass produced by the record companies, by definition non-live, and diffused to the public through numerous retail outlets, traditionally music shops. Records pre-dated radio and television by nearly thirty years, so how were they brought to the attention of the public?

Its members would buy the recorded versions of songs they had heard at the concert hall or music hall or in the cinema; versions of well-known songs that had been passed down through many generations; songs they had encountered through the sale of sheet music for domestic pianos and other instruments; or just the recordings of previously unheard songs that they might sample in the music shop itself. In America, the cradle of modern pop and rock, another important medium existed in the form of the jukebox. Though it scarcely pre-dated radio, it existed alongside the medium and was a familiar feature of the nation's bars, roadhouses and drugstores for a good twenty years before it appeared in other countries.

If these modes of diffusion allow us to describe the commercial manufacture and distribution of records as 'broadcasting' of a kind, we can say that, since the 1940s and 1950s, it has also piggy-backed on a more conventional form of broadcasting by borrowing – and in extreme but numerous cases, monopolising – radio's mode of diffusion. We should of course remember that commercial recordings do not consist only of music: there is also speech content in the form of literary readings, storytellings, comedy and drama. But for three main reasons, such content seems to be much less of a threat to the quiddity and integrity of radio. First, it is much less widespread: while there are scores of all-music stations and networks, very few are dedicated to pre-recorded speech content. Second, and in the UK at least, much of this content *originates* on radio as programme material which is then commercially packaged and sold to the public. Third, speech content also originates in a single performance or event which is some kind of affirmation of the significance of liveness: it is not, as so much modern pop music is, created piecemeal and synthetically in a studio.

Now, however, commercially recorded music is moving on to other and perhaps more effective modes of diffusion, notably the internet and the intensive social networking it generates. At websites such as Amazon and the iTunes Store new albums are publicised and, on a single 'visit', and with just a few clicks of a mouse, can be sampled, purchased and downloaded. Moreover the internet hosts a number of proprietary music services such as Spotify, Deezer and Grooveshark which stream a vast selection of music to the public from a multitude of major and independent labels. As well as from the direct sale of their music, the labels make their money from the licensing fees and royalties paid to them by the services; the services make theirs from the advertising and listener subscriptions they attract. Music is even being publicised on the websites of companies whose main business interests lie elsewhere. Urban Outfitters primarily sells fashionable clothing brands, with smaller departments dedicated to homeware and CDs, but its website offers free playlists for its youthful customers to listen to online while browsing through its products. The idea is that, whether on Facebook or Twitter or by old-fashioned word of mouth, they will then share their knowledge of new music and stimulate sales. It is hard to think that all these developments will fail to have an impact on traditional sound broadcasting, if only over the longer term (Rudin, 2011, p. 66).

Let me summarise the argument I have been making and the issues it raises. At about the time it was being eclipsed by the rise of television, radio largely gave itself over to the promotion of commercially pre-recorded music, but there is now a risk that this music might abandon it for newer and more effective platforms – or at least make much less use of it than hitherto. If this happens, the exponents of the public-service philosophy will be vindicated, but perhaps in a deeper way than they realise. Their objection to recorded all-music radio was twofold. First, it would reduce the general cultural resource of broadcasting to a sales-pitch, and for just one kind of content; second, instead of affording content that the public could not obtain, or obtain easily, from elsewhere, it would merely provide what the public had always been able to acquire from other sources. However, a third objection is that the pop music, of which most all-music radio consists of, is fundamentally at odds with broadcasting of any kind. Historically, broadcasting's unique quality and *raison d'être* is the live representation of what exists naturally or objectively or autonomously, whereas modern pop records differ from most other kinds of recording in their refusal to acknowledge any coherent and originating principle of liveness. They do not capture a performance that occurred in 'the real world' but are concocted in a studio from a number of separate vocal and instrumental tracks and a whole range of technological enhancements.

If radio were to be abandoned by pre-recorded pop music – something which might happen only over the longer term – we might expect it to return to its pristine focus on liveness, or, if the material it broadcasts is pre-recorded (and we have seen why this must so often happen), on material which is at least *capable* of live performance. But this probably means that it will carry less pop music, even by artists who are looking to promote their records, because as we have seen, the live performance of pop mostly falls short of the quality that the records achieve. If radio's inherent suitability to live or as-live music is going to be exploited in the future, it is more likely to be in terms of jazz, classical and folk than electronically mediated pop, and this would make it a much less commercial and thus less popular medium than formerly.

Nevertheless, the change of function would achieve two things, and to understand them better we need to remind ourselves that liveness has significance only within a culture in which recording is prevalent. Let us imagine that we are back in a time when there was not only no electronic capture of sounds and images but no mechanical capture of words – no writing or printing (for these too are forms of recording). We would then be in a *pre-literate* age. Since there would be almost no mediated or 'second-hand' experience, almost nothing to measure liveness against, there could be no special sense of it: liveness is simply all there is. Yet I say 'almost' because in pre-literate times, there existed bards and minstrels who recited poems and sang songs from memory – and what is memory if not a recording and playback device? Recording is not something that is purely technical. By design or accident, these bards and minstrels undoubtedly introduced variations in, and departures from, the material they had learned from their predecessors, but in large part, it did not originate with them. In a certain sense, it consisted of 'recordings' and we are reminded that the live and the recorded are inextricably mixed.

We should also remind ourselves that there is an important 'pre-recorded' element in dramatic and musical performances that we conventionally regard as live. In what we call live theatre, the actors are likely to be relaying a script that they have memorised: in music concerts other than for highly improvisatory forms like jazz, the musicians have a score – and even most kinds of jazz include some pre-scripted element. Indeed, we could go so far as to say that any communication that is not spontaneous is not live, for it will merely be an expression of something that has been planned or premeditated: there are things within it that belong to another time. Nevertheless, we prize the live aspects of these performances so highly – the tangible presence of the performers, the countless inventive and impromptu elaborations that they introduce into whatever 'script' they are following – that we overlook the premeditated aspect and simply call them 'live'. What is the attraction of liveness? Why have certain forms of drama and music remained curiously resistant to recording?

In Chapter 3, we mentioned the need for co-presence between performers and audiences, especially on the part of the latter. Yet in a culture which is dominated by recording, whether in the form of newspapers, books, films or sound files, there is a further attraction: despite the pre-scripting, every performance is, in all its merits and flaws, *unique*. While it is unfolding, its course and conclusion are unknowable, and it is precious precisely because it is uncapturable and irrecoverable. It has defied replication, whether in the form of a single recording that can be played and replayed repeatedly or one that can be turned into countless copies of itself. After it finishes, nothing remains.

In future, radio could perhaps exploit this attraction, for, even if much of its music would of necessity be pre-recorded and only transmitted *as if* live, the very fact that it is the reflection of a true performance and intended for broadcast rather than mass production and public purchase would be sufficient. Hence, radio's first achievement would be to strengthen music's ancient affinity with theatre. Historically, both are *live* genres in the sense that their audiences have paid for something ephemeral – for admission to an event – and not for any artefact, such as a film or sound recording, that the event leaves. Once it has concluded, they will be obliged to share their experience of it with nobody. And radio's second achievement would be to revive the original, essentially public-service idea of broadcasting as a means of providing for the general public what is otherwise unavailable to it – in this case the uniqueness of a particular performance.

Nevertheless, when we reflect that sound broadcasting, whose great innovation was liveness, has for so long surrendered itself to the promotion of pre-recorded commercial music, we are reminded that prediction is risky – especially one as utopian as this!

6 Television and Recording (2): Enhancing Liveness

So far we have been looking at types of recording which, whatever their semblance of liveness, are separate from the present either because, like cinema films and many pre-fabricated television programmes, they were evidently created prior to transmission; or because, like soap operas, they depict a parallel fictional world which has no genuine connection to the world of real time. They are *substitutes* for live programming.

We must now consider two other kinds of recording which in their different ways seek to *enhance* liveness by aspiring to be part of the present, or at least be in a more direct relationship to it, their purpose being to help us understand it more clearly. Both are highly topical: they exist within a 'zone of liveness' because, if they are not transmitted and viewed soon after the occurrence of the events they capture, they will cease to be of value (Kavka and West, 2004, p. 140). The first of these is typified by news actuality, the short film clips that are dropped into news bulletins, or by programmes that show highlights of recent sporting events. As Jérôme Bourdon (2000, pp. 544–5) points out, the news contains a paradox: in order to be credible it must be broadcast live, yet much of the actuality it uses has been recorded. In fact, news programmes are often characterised by two different times – that of the film clips they contain, which were shot in the recent past, and the live context and simultaneous commentary provided by the newsreader or correspondent. The effect is to absorb the past into a kind of expanded present, the images seeming to be part of the same moment as the live asseverations of the news staff.

The interplay of liveness and recording is even more interesting in sports programmes. Live sports coverage is nothing less than news in the making, for, unlike conventional news broadcasts, which for the most part give a live account of events that have recently happened, its events are unfolding before our eyes and will have an unknown outcome: television's liveness could not be more potently illustrated. On the other hand, the desire of sporting bodies to protect the revenues they derive from stadium attendances and pay-TV channels means that the viewers of generalist, free-to-air networks mostly experience these sports in the form of recorded 'highlights'. A famous example is BBC 1's *Match of the Day* (1964–), which shows abridged versions of premier football matches on Saturday evenings, several hours after they have been played. These highlights are embedded into a live studio programme with a presenter and two pundits, who discuss each match at its conclusion and review bits of the recorded material to illustrate the points they have been making. (It is conceivable that on certain occasions the programme is *not* live, for there is an opportunity to pre-record it at some point between the end of the matches at 4.45 pm and the transmission of the programme at about 10.15 pm. But pre-recording would be risky, for some of the matches could have conse-quences – the resignation of a manager or an update on the injury of a star player – which might not occur until the time of the transmission.)

Yet, whether or not the programme itself is live, what is interesting about *Match of the Day* is the way in which the matches it features afford the viewer a kind of make-believe and recurrent liveness. What she typi-cally does is to treat the programme as a time machine, taking herself back a few hours to the moment of the kick-off. For the purposes of vividness, it is a common human impulse to abolish temporal differ-ences, to pretend to be back in the past or, more often, to imagine that past events are taking place in the here and now. The latter impulse is sometimes apparent in our use of language, specifically when we replace the past tense with the so-called vivid present: 'So as I walked out of the carpark, this policeman comes up to me and asks me what I think I'm doing.' However, in *Match of the Day*, the images of daylight, which we are watching at night – images which are accompanied not by scripted reports couched in the past tense but by live commentary – mean that it is more probable that the viewer will imagine herself back in the past: and since several matches are featured, she is able to do it repeatedly.

To fully achieve this pretence she must, of course, remain ignorant of the results, for in order to recreate our present in the past we must remain ignorant of the future that has now become the present! The news bulletin which usually precedes *Match of the Day* will often announce the big results (for sport is not only entertainment but news), and so those viewers who wish to watch the programme are invited to preserve their ignorance by 'looking away now'. What I am suggesting, then, is, that even though almost all of their content has been pre-recorded, there is a topicality about programmes like *Match of the Day* which allows them to be regarded as live. Indeed, if the viewer watches on a time-shift basis (a practice about which we will have more to say shortly), the zone of liveness could be extended – conceivably, if she can shun the next day's media and the tactless tongues of friends, for twenty-four hours or so. Much beyond that, however, the programmes would no longer serve the purpose of live-seemingness.

There is a second kind of recording whose aim is to use the past to enhance the present, and it is one that is usually an element *within* a programme, whether live or recorded, rather than a whole programme in itself. This is the 'instant' or action replay. We noted in Chapter 4 that when Ampex video technology arrived in the mid-1950s and enabled the TV networks to pre-record their programmes, its great innovation was nevertheless the instant-replay facility – which was put to immediate use in the coverage of sport. There is a sense in which the instant replay and the technology that made it possible are now of merely historical interest. Unlike conventional film, videotape required no processing and was instantly viewable: hence it could be used within the live coverage of sport to reprise an incident as soon as it had occurred and then allow a rapid return to the live action. During the subsequent decades, not only was video used increasingly in television production but its successor, digital technology, offered the same immediate (re)viewability. Nevertheless, as originated by video, the instant replay introduced a feature into live coverage, especially of sport, that has remained crucial ever since.

In programmes of sporting highlights such as *Match of the Day*, it is often incorporated into the post-match analysis, but I wish to focus here on its use *within* the coverage of a match which is live or 'as-live' – that is, being recorded in its entirety for a later transmission which might consist of the whole match but more probably of edited highlights. The instant-replay facility can rerun an event exactly as it occurred and can also speed up the event, something that is normally done to remind the viewer of the context: but what it does to greatest effect is, of course, slow down the event. It is a striking reminder that recording offers us a way not only of abridging and shortening time but, almost metaphysically, of *expanding* it (Lury, 2005, pp. 95–6, 116). Just as crucially, television uses it in such a way as to persuade us that *nothing of the subsequent events has been lost*. Hence, the phenomenology of the instant replay is complex and we must now do our best to unpick it.

Its first aim is to enable us to observe and understand an event that would otherwise be too quick and complex for us to capture. Indeed, we are well aware that a consequence of instant-replay technology has been not only to illuminate sporting techniques and prowess but to call into question some of the decisions made by the unaided eyes of umpires and referees (Briggs, 1995, pp. 837–8). Video capture is now used to assist decisions in a number of sports, notably cricket, tennis and athletics. Football has been resistant but this could change as a result of the match between England and Germany in the 2010 World Cup, when the referee's refusal to allow a goal because he thought that the ball had not crossed the line was shown by the instant replay to have been erroneous.

The instant replay is extraordinarily vivid yet its non-liveness, the presence of technological mediation, is blatant. Its speed is seldom natural: it is either shorter or, more often, longer than the duration of the event itself, and sometimes graphics are superimposed on the images. Part of an image may be highlighted or a ball's trajectory may be traced: an area of the pitch is sometimes shaded in order to determine whether a player was offside at the moment a ball was being played. Yet it also displays some of the characteristics of liveness or near-liveness. Its images are as fluid and dynamic as those of conventional film, but seem even more lifelike because their sequence is unedited in the sense of being unabridged: and they are 'larger than life' in enabling us to see more of an event, or at least to see it more meaningfully, than we ever could either as spectators who are physically present or by watching continuous live television.

However, the second role of the instant replay is every bit as important: to allow us to return to the real time of the match as quickly as possible and thus reassure us that we have missed nothing of the events that follow, whether they are being shown live or recorded for later transmission. It is thus an attempt to have it both ways, to freeze a moment in order to help us understand it more clearly yet to suggest that there has been no interruption in the temporal flow of the broadcast. Indeed, there is a sense in which this is strictly true, for as Stephanie Marriott (2007, p. 79) points out, the instant replay does not involve a suspension of the present but the use of the past to accompany the present. How so? It is usually characterised by a bifurcation between the commentator's words and the images we can see; the commentary and the ambient sounds of the match continue to be live – in real time – even though the commentary presently refers to the re-run images of the action replay. Hence, the 'past' of the replay is embedded within the continuing present of the broadcast and indeed, because of this temporal ambiguity, the commentator's analysis sometimes vacillates between the past and present tenses (Marriott, 2007, p. 80–2). Yet it also offers us the reassurance that we are not missing any subsequent events of importance and that, if there is a risk that we might, we will instantly return to live pictures. For these various reasons – the revelations of the replayed slow-motion images, the fast return to live action, and indeed, the fact that we have never really left it – we might describe the effect of the instant replay as one of *hyper*-liveness. At the very least, the instant replay seems to strengthen rather than undermine television's claim to be a live medium (Feuer, 1983, p. 15).

We will conclude this discussion with a glance at the temporal complexities that liveness and recording can involve. We noted that, while the viewer is watching an instant replay during the live transmission of a football match, she is inhabiting two times at once: the time of the replay itself, which is also the time of the commentator's words and the point that the match has presently reached; and the time, probably only a few moments earlier, that the replayed event originally occurred. However, if the transmission is of a pre-recorded match, the viewer will be inhabiting three times. First, there is the time of the transmission – the time at which she is watching. Second, there is the current time within the match – that is, the time of the commentary which accompanies the instant replay and of the continuing events in the match that are not presently visible to the viewer. And third, there is the past time within the match – that of the event now being reviewed in the instant replay. If, however, the viewer is watching the match on a time-shifted basis, *four* times are involved. I might, for instance, be watching on Sunday morning between 9.30 and 11.00 an off-air recording of *Match of the Day* transmitted the previous evening between 10.15 and 11.45, but of a game which took place and was pre-recorded that afternoon between 3.00 and 4.45.

Ten minutes after the kick-off, a goal was scored – that is, at 3.10 pm – and for clarity's sake let us suppose that those first ten minutes appear in the programme without any abridgement. Two minutes after it is scored, the goal is re-run within the transmitted programme as an instant replay. Four times are thus collapsed into one – the time of the viewing, the time of the transmission, the time of the replay and the time of the goal – for at 9.42 on Sunday morning I am watching a transmission that took place at 10.27 the previous evening of an instant replay that was run at 3.12 that afternoon of an event that actually occurred at 3.10. In a later chapter we shall have more to say about the implications of time-shift viewing and listening.

7 Real Time and Reel Time: An Evening's Programmes on BBC 1

In this chapter, I hope to reveal more about the typical yet complex relationship between liveness and recording in modern television by exploring a single evening's programmes on one of the most popular networks in the UK. The programmes were transmitted between 6.00 pm and 12.25 am on BBC 1 on Tuesday, 15 June 2010, and the regional news bulletins that are included are northern because at the time of the transmission I happened to be in North-East England. However, my viewing experience of BBC 1 would have been very similar to that of viewers in any and every other part of the country: the regional bulletins are broadcast at fixed times in the schedule and in identical formats, while the rest of the programmes are common to all regions.

In my description of the schedule I have used "L" to signify Live and "R" to signify (pre-) Recorded, but I should make three initial points. The first is that, while the reader will soon realise that within certain of the programmes live and recorded elements are often intermingled, I have accorded each programme a kind of generic status. Thus, while there are lots of film clips in the news bulletins I have given them the generic description 'live' (L). Second, not only are liveness and recording often intermingled: it is sometimes impossible to tell whether what one is watching or hearing is one or the other, a point I will return to in the subsequent analysis. Finally, each moment of a television transmission is extremely 'busy' and multilayered: to capture every detail is slow and arduous, and despite my best efforts there may be important visual or acoustic elements that I have overlooked. Some readers may be reluctant to plod through my description from beginning to end, but even a cursory reading should convince them of the complex roles of liveness and recording in television.

6.00 pm NEWS AND WEATHER (L)

Sounds	Images
VO: 'This is BBC One in the North East and Cumbria. Now the BBC News with George Alagiah and Jeff Brown at six o'clock.' (L) Music bed: BBC News theme (R)	Network ident: footage of people flying kites followed by graphic 'BBC One NE and Cumbria' (R)
The Prime Minister's reactions in the House of Commons to the findings of the Bloody Sunday inquiry (R). Music bed continues (R)	The Prime Minister at the Dispatch Box addressing the members of the House (R)
Newsreader George Alagiah explains (L) the Prime Minister's apology. Music bed continues (R)	Newsreader in studio (L)
Newsreader's VO (L) followed by the statements of the relatives and reactions of the crowd (R). Music bed continues (R)	Relatives of the victims of Bloody Sunday addressing a public rally in Northern Ireland (R)
VO from newsreader (L). Music bed continues (R)	Historic footage of Bloody Sunday riots (1972) (R)
Newsreader sets out a key issue raised by the inquiry and, while the music bed continues (R), reads the other headlines (L):	Newsreader in studio (L)
• The oil disaster in the Gulf of Mexico (L)	• Shots of US congressmen (R)
• Rupert Murdoch's bid to control BSkyB (L)	• Banks of TV monitors and Sky logo (R)
• Princes William and Harry are touring Africa (L)	• The two princes hoisting a snake onto their shoulders (R)
Music bed continues (R)	
While music bed continues (R), newsreader Jeff Brown previews the main stories in the North East (L):	Newsreader in *Look North* studio (L)
• Funerals have taken place of victims of Cumbrian mass killer Derek Bird (L)	• Shots of funeral and still photographs of two of the victims (R)
• Racehorse trainer is terrorised by robbers (L)	• Filmed reconstruction of incident from *Crimewatch* (R)
Music bed continues (R)	

Sounds	Images
BBC News theme music swells to a conclusion (R)	Sequence of graphics of the world and the BBC logo (R)
Newsreader bids us good evening and returns to the main story, the Bloody Sunday inquiry (L). He cues a report from a correspondent in Northern Ireland	Newsreader in studio (L)
Correspondent's VO (R)	Historic footage (1972) of Bloody Sunday riots (R)
The Prime Minister's words in the House of Commons (R)	The Prime Minister at the Dispatch Box in the House of Commons (R)
Correspondent's VO (R) on the sound-track of street fighting (R)	More footage (1972) of Bloody Sunday riots (R)
More of the Prime Minister's words in the House of Commons (R)	The Prime Minister at the Dispatch Box (R)
Correspondent's VO frames the public statements of the victims' relatives and the reactions of the crowd (R)	Shots of the victims' relatives and the crowds at the public rally in Northern Ireland (R)
Newsreader (L) cues a report from defence correspondent, Caroline Wyatt	Newsreader in studio (L)
Wyatt's VO (R) on 1972 soundtrack of street fighting (R)	More footage (1972) of Bloody Sunday riots (R)
Wyatt's VO cues former head of British Army, Sir Mike Jackson, followed by Jackson's reaction to the findings of the inquiry (R)	Footage of Sir Mike Jackson reading a statement (R)
Wyatt's VO (R) on 1972 soundtrack of street fighting (R)	More footage (1972) of Bloody Sunday riots (R)
Soldiers' lawyer Stephen Pollard impugning some of the findings of the inquiry (R)	Lawyer addressing an unseen interviewer (R)
Wyatt's VO (R) on 1972 soundtrack of street fighting (R)	More footage (1972) of Bloody Sunday riots (R)
Col. Stuart Tootal, former commander of 3 Para, gives a soldier's perspective on the Bloody Sunday riots (R)	Tootal addressing an unseen interviewer (R)
Wyatt's concluding VO (R) on 1972 soundtrack of street fighting (R)	More footage (1972) of Bloody Sunday riots (R)

Sounds	Images
Newsreader cues (L) Daniel Boettscher, who has been gauging the mood in Londonderry	Newsreader in studio (L)
Boettscher's VO on sounds of today's rally (R)	Shots of today's rally (R)
A man who was wounded in the Bloody Sunday shootings gives his reactions to the findings of the inquiry (R)	The man addressing an unseen interviewer (R)
Boettscher's commentary (R)	Shots of the memorial to the victims of Bloody Sunday and still photograph of one of those who was killed (R)
Boettscher's VO on sounds of today's rally (R)	Shots of today's rally (R)
Boettscher continues his report (R)	Boettscher addressing the camera (R)
Reaction to the findings of the inquiry by Unionist MP Gregory Campbell (R)	Campbell addressing an unseen interviewer (R)
Boettscher's VO on sounds of today's rally (R)	More shots of today's rally (R)
Reactions of individuals at the rally and Boettscher's concluding remarks (R)	Individuals addressing an unseen interviewer (R)
Newsreader cues (L) the reaction of Sinn Fein leader Gerry Adams, delivered 'within the last hour', to today's events	Newsreader in studio (L)
Adams's reaction to the findings of the inquiry (R)	Adams addressing an unseen interviewer (R)
Newsreader cues and conducts an interview with political editor Nick Robinson (L)	Newsreader in studio (L) with image of Robinson standing outside 10 Downing Street (L)
Robinson assesses the impact of the findings both on the government and the people of Northern Ireland (L)	Robinson addressing the camera below the caption 'LIVE Downing Street' (L)
Newsreader announces (L) that viewers can get more on the story from the BBC website	Moving graphic of computer and website (R)
Newsreader announces (L) that President Obama is due to address the nation about the effects of the BP oil-spill in the Gulf. From Washington, Steve Kingston reports	Newsreader in studio (L)

Sounds	Images
Kingston's VO on sounds of protest followed by sounds of congressional hearing and intercut with remarks delivered by two congressmen (R)	Shots of protestors outside Congress, followed by film of the hearings (R)
Explanation of hearings by Kingston (R)	Kingston addressing the camera in a Washington street (R)
Kingston's VO on sounds of the seashore (R)	Shots of President Obama on the Gulf coast, inspecting the effects of the oil spill (R)
Kingston's VO intercut with President's remarks (R)	President Obama addressing the troops attempting to clean up the oil spill (R)
Newsreader gives a time check and trails remaining stories in the bulletin (L)	Newsreader in studio (L)
Music bed: BBC News theme (R) under soundtrack of the trophy presentation and including the original commentary (R), followed by newsreader's VO (L) reporting that Franz Beckenbauer has said that England is 'going backwards' at the World Cup	Footage of Beckenbauer receiving the trophy for Germany after a previous World Cup final and holding it aloft (R)
Look North newsreader Jeff Brown promises (L) the latest sport and a weather update, plus …	Newsreader in *Look North* studio (L)
Brown's VO (L) trails a story about the well-kept garden that a pensioner was ordered to dig up. Music bed continues (R)	Film of pensioner working in his garden (R)
Brown's VO trails (L) a sneak preview of the stage version of *Dad's Army*. Music bed continues (R)	Opening graphics of this old TV sitcom (R), followed by shots of the new stage production (R)
Music theme fades up and ends (R). Alagiah announces (L) that Rupert Murdoch's News Corporation is trying to buy up all the remaining shares of BSkyB	Newsreader in the national studio (L)
VO from correspondent Rob Peston (R) with film soundtracks fading in (R)	Still photos of Rupert Murdoch and James Murdoch followed by film of each (R)

Sounds	Images
Peston explains the story of the Murdochs' bid (R)	Peston sitting in front of large TV screen on which various phrases and graphics appear in sequence (R)
Peston's VO asks why News Corporation wishes to own the whole company (R)	Aerial film of BSkyB's headquarters (R)
Explanation by media consultant Steve Hewlett (R)	Hewlett addressing an unseen interviewer (R)
Peston's VO continues with soundtrack fading in from BSkyB's TV studios. He asks whether the competition and media regulators will let the deal through (R)	Film of BSkyB's headquarters, followed by interior shots of TV studios (R)
Remarks from Adrian Sanders, a Liberal Democrat MP, arguing that the Murdoch acquisition would be against the public interest (R)	Sanders addressing an unseen interviewer (R)
Peston's VO over the sounds of the rioters (R)	Historical shots of print unions rioting at Wapping in the mid-1980s (R)
Musical soundtrack (R)	Graphic sequence trailing the launch of Sky TV in 1989 (R)
Peston's VO continues over the sequence (R), near the end of which a TV soundtrack fades in (R)	Still photo of Rupert Murdoch (R) followed by photographic shots of the *Sunday Times* online newspaper (R) and then a montage of TV screens showing BSkyB content with the Sky logo fading in (R)
Newsreader announces (L) that two British soldiers have been killed in Afghanistan and he continues the account as a VO	Newsreader in studio (L) followed by animated map showing the location of the deaths (R)
VO from newsreader: the BNP leader Nick Griffin has been invited to a Buckingham Palace garden party (L)	Shots of Griffin and his followers in the street and entering a car (R)
VO from newsreader: the High Court has quashed an extradition order for a man convicted in his absence of a murder in Italy (L)	Shots of the man and his legal team leaving the High Court (R)

Sounds	Images
Princes Harry and William with a ten-foot python during a tour of Africa (L). Royal correspondent Nicholas Wychell is travelling with them in Botswana	Newsreader in studio (L) with large still photograph of the princes on the screen behind him (R)
Wychell's VO on a soundtrack of noises including the chants of a welcoming choir of women. It finishes as a sound-track to his image (R)	Sequence of the princes walking down a lane, being introduced to various people, and then shouldering the python. The camera then pulls back to Wychell in the foreground, who concludes his piece by addressing it directly (R)
Wychell's concluding VO on the sounds of the princes' visit (R)	Shots of the princes visiting a pen containing two cheetahs (R)
Newsreader announces (L) that Franz Beckenbauer has criticised the performance of the England team at the World Cup. James Pearce reports from the England training base in Rustenburg	Newsreader in the studio (L)
Pearce's VO on soundtrack of England's first match against the US (R)	Film of the England goalkeeper Green conceding an easy goal (R)
Pearce's VO (R) on soundtrack of World Cup presentation	Historic footage of Franz Beckenbauer receiving the World Cup as captain of Germany (R)
Pearce's VO continues (R)	Two contemporary photos of Beckenbauer and a transcript of his remarks (R)
Pearce continues his report (R)	Pearce addressing the camera against the darkened background of Rustenburg (R)
Pearce's VO on soundtrack of the England players' visit intercut with players' remarks (R)	Shots of England players visiting a local orphanage and delivering remarks to an unseen interviewer (R)
Newsreader returns to the evening's main story (L): the findings of the Bloody Sunday inquiry, and gets a final word from correspondent Chris Butler in Londonderry	Newsreader in the studio (L)

Sounds	Images
Newsreader's questions and Butler's responses (L)	Shot of Butler against a background of Londonderry (L)
Newsreader cues weather forecast from Darren Bett (L)	Newsreader in studio and a shot of Bett in the same studio (L)
Bett delivers the weather forecast (L)	Bett addresses the camera (L) against maps of the British Isles and western Europe which display moving graphics (R)
Newsreader delivers the closing headlines (L). The BBC News theme (R) fades up under his words	Newsreader in the studio (L)
Newsreader's VO (L) on soundtrack of crowd noise (R) Music bed continues (R)	A clip of the celebrating crowds in Londonderry (R)
Newsreader introduces the regional news programmes 'where you are' and bids us goodbye (L) Music bed continues (R)	Newsreader in the studio (L)

6.30 pm REGIONAL NEWS (L)

Sounds	Images
The headlines this Tuesday evening (L)	Newsreader Jeff Brown in the *Look North* studio (L)
Newsreader's VO (L) announcing the funeral of two of the victims of Cumbrian mass killer Derek Bird	Shots of coffin being unloaded from a hearse outside a church (R)
Newsreader's VO (L): Support staff of the Cleveland police force are to be contracted out to the private sector. BBC News theme music (R) fades up under VO	Shots of uniformed staff working in an open-plan office (R)
Newsreader's VO (L): Pensioner told by his housing association to grass over his well-kept garden. Music bed continues (R)	Shots of flowery garden and pensioner working in it (R)

Sounds	Images
Newsreader's VO (L): The Queen's English is under siege – what are your pet linguistic hates? Music bed continues (R)	Shots of a street in a town with printed errors of spelling and grammar sliding across the screen (R)
A woman airs her favourite examples of bad English (R) Music bed continues (R)	Shot of woman in street addressing an unseen interviewer (R)
Female sports presenter reports on a 'cracking night of twenty20 cricket in Durham' (L). Music bed continues (R)	Newsreader and sports presenter perched side by side in the studio (L)
Sports presenter's VO (L) trailing her ride with one of Britain's top drivers as a prelude to the touring car championships at Croft. Music bed continues (R)	External and internal shots of car racing round the track (R)
The music bed fades up (R)	Sequence of graphics and local images which make up the BBC *Look North* ident (R). The sequence concludes with a quick shot of both newsreader and sports presenter sitting in the studio (L)
Newsreader returns (L) to the story of the funeral of two of Derek Bird's victims. The theme music swells to a conclusion (R)	Newsreader in the studio (L), behind him photographs (R) of the victims
Alison Freeman reports from Egremont, west Cumbria (R)	Shot moves down from church to Freeman addressing the camera (R)
Freeman's VO on a soundtrack of church-bell and birdsong (R)	Coffin being unloaded from hearse outside church, shots of mourning family and friends (R)
Freeman's VO describes the circumstances of the killing and the couple's standing in the community (R)	Still photograph of two of the victims, a married couple (R)
The local vicar talking about the murdered couple (R)	The local vicar addressing an unseen interviewer (R)
Freeman's VO continues over sound of tolling bell (R)	Images of wreaths and hearses (R)
Freeman concludes the report and begins an account of the funeral of a third victim which took place in the same church (R)	Freeman addressing the camera (R)

Sounds	Images
Freeman's VO on a soundtrack of the hearse (R)	Shot of an arriving hearse (R)
Freeman's VO continues on a soundtrack of birdsong in the churchyard (R)	Still photo of the victim (R) followed by pictures of coffin being loaded into a hearse (R)
Freeman concludes her report (R)	Freeman addressing the camera (R)
The newsreader announces (L) that the robbers of a local racehorse trainer have still not been caught. He cues a report by Gerry Jackson	Newsreader in the studio (L)
Jackson's VO (R) over a soundtrack of the *Crimewatch* reconstruction (R), which includes noises and background music	Footage of the *Crimewatch* reconstruction mixed with shots of the actual scenes of the robbery and police combing the area (R)
The newsreader runs through the upcoming stories:	Newsreader in the studio (L)
• The pensioner ordered to turf over his garden (L)	
• The mole population is increasing (L)	Footage of a mole digging underground (R)
Music jingle (R)	Sequence of graphics and local images which make up the BBC *Look North* ident (R)
A soldier who had recently returned from Afghanistan is attacked and killed in a street in Teesside (L). Latanya Shannon reports on his funeral	Newsreader in the studio (L) with a photograph of the victim behind him (R)
Shannon's VO on soundtrack of the footage of the street (R)	Full-screen photograph of the victim followed by film footage of the street in which the victim was attacked (R)
Shannon's VO (R)	Still photographs of soldier with wife and son and of soldier alone (R)
The newsreader announces (L) a coroner's request in respect of the death of another soldier	Newsreader in the studio (L) with a photograph of a second soldier behind him
Newsreader's VO (L)	Full-screen photograph of the soldier followed by film of funeral plaques and a still photograph of the soldier with his family (R)

Sounds	Images
Newsreader announces (L) that plans have been approved to transfer about 500 civilian employees of Cleveland Police to a private company	Newsreader in the studio (L), photograph in background (R)
'Stuart Wincup is in Middlesbrough for us now' (L)	Wincup appears on screen behind newsreader (L)
Wincup delivers his report (L)	Wincup on full screen with Middlesbrough street scene behind (L)
Wincup's report continues as a VO (R) on a soundtrack (R) of the accompanying film footage, followed by a VO (R) from a representative of the staff's trade union	Film of police activity on the streets followed by footage of support staff working in a large office (R)
The representative continues his observations (R)	Shot of union representative addressing an unseen interviewer (R)
Wincup's VO resumes (R)	Film of CCTV images and further staff activity in the office (R)
Wincup's report continues (R)	Wincup addressing the camera against the background of a police-station wall, on which various statistics are projected as a kind of graphic rolling text (R)
A new voice, that of the chairman of the Cleveland Police Authority, is heard as a VO (R) on bed of office sounds (R)	More shots of the support-staff office (R)
The chairman of the Authority continues his remarks (R)	Open-air shot of chairman addressing an unseen interviewer (R)
Wincup's VO resumes (R)	More shots of police activity on the streets (R)
Wincup concludes his report (L)	Wincup with Middlesbrough street scene behind (L)
Newsreader trails (L) an upcoming item in the bulletin – plus:	Newsreader in the studio (L)
• A trail from the actor Leslie Grantham (R)	Film of Grantham addressing the camera (R)
• A trail from the sports correspondent at the Croft Racetrack (R)	Shot of the sports correspondent addressing the camera, with a sports car racing past in the background (R)

Sounds	Images
Music jingle (R)	Sequence of graphics and local images which make up the BBC *Look North* ident (R)
Newsreader introduces (L) a story about a Durham pensioner who was ordered to dig up his garden by the local housing association. Joanne Carter reports	Newsreader in the studio (L), photograph in background (R)
Carter's VO (R)	Shots of pensioner tending his garden (R)
Pensioner's reactions to the order (R)	Shot of pensioner addressing an unseen interviewer (R)
Carter's VO resumes (R)	Shots of the pensioner's house and garden and of him tending his plants (R)
Remarks of housing association representative (R)	Shot of representative addressing an unseen interviewer (R)
Pensioner's remarks, first as a VO and then to the interviewer (R)	Shots of pensioner in the garden and then addressing an unseen interviewer (R)
Carter concludes her report (R)	Final shot of garden (R)
Newsreader introduces an item (L) about the rise in the local mole population. Phil Lavelle reports from rural Northumberland	Newsreader in the studio (L), photo-graph in the background (R)
Lavelle begins his report on a soundtrack of the neighbourhood (R)	Shot of a molehill which then tracks up to Lavelle addressing the camera: brief filmed insert of a mole digging underground (R)
Lavelle introduces a local mole-catcher (R)	Both Lavelle and mole-catcher in shot, with the camera closing in on the latter (R)
The interview continues over local soundtrack (R)	Library pictures of a mole digging underground (R)
The interview continues over local soundtrack (R)	Shots of the mole-catcher and the molehills at his feet (R)
Lavelle thanks the mole-catcher and continues his report (R)	Camera pulls away from mole-catcher and focuses on Lavelle, who addresses it directly (R)

Sounds	Images
Lavelle concludes his report (R)	Final travelling shot of molehills in a field (R)
Newsreader introduces (L) a feature on the use and misuse of the Queen's English. Chris Stewart reports	Newsreader in the studio (L)
Stewart's VO (R) on a piano bed (R)	Shots of a Hexham street on to which moving print is superimposed, illustrating common grammatical errors (R)
Stewart's questions on a bed of street noises (R) and a snatch of the theme music from *Mastermind* (R)	Intercut shots of several interviewees in the street, discussing the errors that most annoy them, and one of them attempting to answer a spelling question (R)
Stewart continues his report on common linguistic errors (R)	Stewart sitting in Hexham town square and addressing the camera directly (R)
Stewart asking a question on a bed of piano music and street noises. His voice continues as a VO, introducing an interview with Rhea Williams of the Queen's English Society (R)	Shot of another interviewee in the street which pulls back to include Stewart (R)
Williams's remarks on the state of English: office noises in the background (R)	Williams in office addressing an unseen interviewer (R)
Stewart going through more common linguistic errors on a bed of town noises and piano music. He punctuates his own remarks with a VO that concludes his report (R)	Stewart sitting in the town square and talking as if to himself. Picture shrinks to zero (R)
Back announcement on the language feature (L)	Newsreader in the studio (L)
Newsreader promotes a debate on 'your pet hates' on tomorrow's breakfast programmes on BBC local radio (L)	A graphic including the names and wavelengths of all the BBC local radio stations in the region (R)
Newsreader introduces the sports stories and exchanges a few words with sports presenter Dawn Thewlis (L)	Newsreader and sports presenter sitting side by side in the studio (L)

Sounds	Images
Thewlis reports on last night's twenty20 cricket match at Durham and cues reporter Katie Gornall (L)	Full shot of Thewlis (L)
Gornall's VO over the sound actuality of the match, which seems to include some broadcast commentary (R)	Footage of the match (R)
Thewlis reports (L) on rumours that the Darlington manager Simon Davey may be leaving the club	Thewlis in the studio (L), followed by shots of Simon Davey walking inside Darlington's stadium (R)
Ex-footballer Paul Gascoigne has been involved in a car accident (L)	Thewlis in the studio (L), followed by footage of Gascoigne at a book-signing (R)
The British touring-car championship will shortly take place at Croft in North Yorkshire. Thewlis cues the story of her ride round the circuit with top driver Jason Plato (L)	Thewlis in the studio (L), with film on the screen behind her showing cars racing round a track (R)
Thewlis's VO (R) on bed of racetrack noises (R)	Cars racing round the Croft circuit (R)
Plato's account of the problems he has had with his car, addressed to the interviewer but partly used as a VO (R)	Plato standing by the racetrack addressing an unseen interviewer, followed by footage of cars racing (R)
Thewlis's VO (R) on a bed of racetrack noises (R)	Cars racing round the track (R)
Plato continues his account of the problems with the car (R)	Plato by the racetrack addressing the unseen interviewer (R)
Thewlis's VO (R) alternating with Plato's VO (R) on a bed of racetrack noises. Trumpet music fades in (R)	Footage of racetrack activity, including shots of Thewlis and Plato greeting one another (R)
Plato's commentary and Thewlis's cries on a bed of car noises and dramatic music (R)	Shots of Plato and Thewlis riding round the circuit (R)
Thewlis's remarks on bed of car noises and music (R)	Car comes to a halt, Thewlis makes a hasty exit (R)
Thewlis concludes the item as a VO (R) on a bed of car noises and music (R)	Cars racing round the Croft circuit (R)
Banter (L) between Thewlis and the newsreader	Thewlis and the newsreader sitting together in the studio (L)

Sounds	Images
Over the sitcom's theme tune (R), the newsreader introduces (L) an item about a new stage version of the TV sitcom *Dad's Army*. Thewlis (L) then cues the report	Newsreader and Thewlis in the studio (L) and on the screen behind them the opening graphics of the TV sitcom (R)
Soundtrack of *Dad's Army* clip, on which the reporter's VO (R) is occasionally heard	Clip from the TV sitcom *Dad's Army* (R)
Actor Leslie Grantham being interviewed by the reporter (R)	Shots of Grantham making up for the stage version of the show and being interviewed. Occasional shots of the reporter/interviewer (R)
Soundtrack from the stage version of the show (R)	Clip of the stage version of the show (R)
Soundtrack from the TV version of the show (R)	Clip of the TV version of the show (R)
Interview with actor Timothy Kightley, who plays the part of Captain Mainwaring (R)	Kightley addressing the unseen interviewer (R)
Reporter's VO (R) on a bed of theatrical dialogue (R)	Clip of the stage version of the show (R)
Newsreader concludes the item and introduces the weather forecaster Paul Mooney (L)	Studio shot of the newsreader and Dawn Thewlis sitting together and the weather forecaster standing beside a screen containing the BBC Weather graphic (L)
Mooney's weather forecast (L)	Full shot of Mooney and the screen (L) containing moving weather graphics and still photographs submitted by viewers (R)
Brown concludes the show (L) as the *Look North* theme music fades in (R)	Studio shot of Mooney, Thewlis and Brown (L) then the concluding BBC *Look North* graphics (R)

- *Over a filmed BBC logo a VO, probably L, introduces the next programme,* EastEnders *(1985–)*
- *A VO, probably R, accompanies a filmed trailer for* Imagine *(2003–), a BBC 1 arts programme which tonight at 10.30 pm will feature violinist Nigel Kennedy*
- *A VO, probably R, accompanies a promotion consisting of clips and graphics of the BBC World Cup Online*

- *A VO, probably R, accompanies a promotion consisting of clips and graphics for Radio 1 Live Music*
- *A VO, probably R, accompanies a trailer consisting of clips and graphics for a forthcoming episode of* Doctor Who *(2005–) on BBC 1*

7.00 pm EASTENDERS (R)

Over the introductory music and images of *EastEnders* (1985–), a VO, probably L, trails *Holby City* (1999–), which is coming up in an hour's time.

In the episode itself, there are occasional background images of England flags, pennants and soccer posters evidently meant to evoke the nation's contemporary World Cup campaign.

As the credits roll at the end of the programme, a VO, probably L, trails *Holby City*, the next programme on BBC 1, together with a romantic film comedy on BBC 3.

BBC 1 logo and musical jingle (R)
Ninety-second news update with Ellie Crisell, who is seen and heard L throughout. Behind her is a screen, which shows the following – all R.

1) *Footage of Bloody Sunday, which occurred in 1972, followed by today's rally in Londonderry, including sound actuality, at which the findings of the inquiry were announced.*
2) *Children's farms need tougher regulation after an e-coli outbreak. Footage of farm animals.*
3) *Barack Obama is visiting the Gulf states which are affected by the oil-spill. Pictures, with sound actuality, of the President on a beach.*
4) *BNP leader Nick Griffin has been invited to a Buckingham Palace garden party. Shots of Griffin with sound actuality.*
5) *Princes Harry and William are visiting Africa. Shots of them hoisting a snake on to their shoulders, together with sound actuality.*

Newsreader Latanya Shannon reads the latest from Look North. *She is seen and heard L throughout. Behind her is a screen showing the BBC logo (R) and then the following – all R.*

1) *Shots of the funerals of three more of Derek Bird's victims combined with still photographs. No soundtrack.*
2) *Civilian staff at Cleveland Police are being transferred to employment with a private company. Footage of staff working in an open-plan office. No soundtrack.*
3) *Tomorrow's weather: full-screen map of northern England with moving graphics.*

- *Over a filmed BBC logo a VO, probably L, introduces the next programme,* Holby City
- *A VO, probably R, accompanies a filmed trailer for* Crimewatch *(1984–) on this evening at 9.00 pm*
- *A trailer (R) for* Lee Nelson's 'Well Good' Show *(2010) on BBC 3 this Thursday*
- *A VO, probably R, accompanies a filmed trailer for the current BBC 2 series,* Tribal Wives *(2008–)*
- *A trailer, including a VO and music bed, for the forthcoming coverage on BBC 2 and Five Live of the Wimbledon tennis tournament (R)*
- *Over the BBC logo (R) a VO, probably L, introduces ...*

8.00 pm HOLBY CITY (R)

The opening sequence of images and credits is followed by a 'retrospective trailer' (R), whose purpose is to remind the viewer of what has already happened in the serial. There is no way of knowing whether this trailer was assembled before or after the present episode was recorded, but it strengthens the illusion that the current episode is, indeed, in the present: live.

On the other hand, like that of *EastEnders*, the tight, crisp sequence of scenes in different locations implies that the programme has been pre-recorded.

As the credits roll at the end of the programme, a VO, probably L, trails the next programmes on BBC 1, 2 and 4.

- *A trailer (R) consisting of clips for new drama coming soon on BBC 1*
- *A trailer (R) for the Radio 4 science programme* Material World, *consisting of an actor delivering a monologue direct to camera, but with a concluding VO, probably also R*
- *Trailer (R) of clips for a programme about sopranos on BBC next Saturday; concludes with a VO, probably also R*
- *BBC 1 ident (R) of helicopter hovering over lighthouse; VO (L) introduces ...*

9.00 pm CRIMEWATCH (L)

Sounds	Images
Narrator's VO (L?) on bed of *Crimewatch* theme music and sounds of a murderous assault (R)	Re-enactment of the assault on a sixty-eight-year-old grandfather, followed by a still photograph of the victim (R)
On bed of theme music, remarks of the victim's son (R)	Man addressing unseen interviewer (R)

Sounds	Images
Crimewatch theme music (R)	Sequence of images and graphics introducing the programme (R)
Music fades under the opening remarks (L) of programme presenter Kirsty Young	Shots of the studio and the programme presenter (L)
Sounds of a burglary and assault followed by the words of the victim (R)	Snatch of dramatic re-enactment of an armed burglary and assault in County Durham followed by victim addressing an unseen interviewer (R)
Young introduces (L) her two co-presenters, Rav and Matthew, who trail crimes and criminals that will be featured later in the programme (L)	Shots of Rav and Matthew in different parts of the studio (L)
Young opens the first item (L): the murder of sixty-eight-year-old Barry Rubery	Young in studio, addressing camera (L), photograph of victim in background (R)
Soundtrack of reconstruction over bed of dramatic music (R)	Filmed reconstruction of friend finding Rubery's body (R)
Music fades under Matthew's narration (R)	Matthew in the victim's village, walking towards the camera (R)
Music resumes (R)	Still photograph of Rubery (R)
Music held under remarks of Rubery's daughter and son (R)	Separate shots of daughter and son addressing unseen interviewer, intercut with still photographs of victim (R)
Music (R) held under Matthew's VO (L). Some background location sounds (R)	Shots of Rubery's house and of actor who bears a resemblance to him moving around the property (R)
Music (R) held under remarks of daughter and son (R)	Shots of daughter and son addressing unseen interviewer, intercut with still photographs of victim (R)
Matthew's VO (L) recounts a meeting on the day of the killing between Rubery and a friend. Location sounds and dialogue. Music bed continues (R)	Filmed reconstruction of meeting between Rubery and friend (R)
Matthew's VO (L): later in the day, Rubery went out to a social event with some friends. Location sounds and dialogue (R). Music bed continues (R)	Filmed reconstruction of social event: Rubery chatting with some friends over a meal (R)

Sounds	Images
Matthew's VO (L): eyewitness accounts of a Land Rover parked that evening outside Rubery's home. Location sounds and dialogue (R). Music bed continues (R)	Shots of parked Land Rover followed by reconstruction of Rubery's return home (R)
Matthew's VO (L) continues, bracketing location sounds of the assault (R). Music bed continues (R)	Reconstruction of the assault on Rubery on the path leading to his back door, followed by brief shot of Matthew in Rubery's yard (R)
Rubery's daughter and then his son recount their feelings when told of their father's death (R). Music bed (R)	Separate shots of daughter and son addressing unseen interviewer, followed by still photograph of Rubery (R)
Interview by Matthew of the detective investigating the case (R). Location sounds and music bed (R)	Aerial shots of Rubery's property, followed by Matthew and officer at the scene of the murder, intercut with clips of the reconstructed assault and subsequent burglary of the house, photographs of property that was stolen and a still image of the house (R)
Young interviews the investigating officer about some new information that has emerged and leads that the police wish to follow. She then introduces Rav (L)	Programme presenter in the studio, who turns to talk to the investigating officer (L). Interview intercut with shots of stolen property (R)
Rav describes each of the individuals who are wanted on various matters by the police. Background of studio noise (L)	Rav stands before a photogallery of people who are wanted by the police (L)
Young introduces the case of Howard Johnson, a racehorse trainer who was the victim of an armed assault and burglary (L)	Presenter in studio, addressing camera (L)
Narrative by Johnson himself (R), mostly as a VO but with some remarks in interview, and both over soundtrack of reconstruction and bed of dramatic music (R)	Reconstruction of the incident, combining shots of racehorses galloping, Johnson's talking head addressing an unseen interviewer, the farm and surrounding countryside, still photographs, and a re-enactment of the attack itself (R)

Sounds	Images
Young interviews the detective investigating the case against a background of studio noise (L)	Presenter and detective talking in the studio (L), punctuated by still photographs of Johnson and his wife and of a car thought to be used in the assault (R)
Young concludes the item, appeals to viewers for information and introduces Rav with tonight's CCTV footage (L)	Presenter in studio, addressing camera (L)
Rav introduces his report (L)	Rav addresses camera and then turns to a studio screen (L)
Rav's VO (L) on a bed of dramatic music (R)	A sequence of crimes captured on CCTV (R)
Music (R) fades into studio noises (L). Rav concludes his report with an appeal for information (L)	Rav standing beside the studio screen and addressing the camera (L)
Young introduces an item about the theft of a lorryload of England football shirts (L)	Presenter in studio, addressing camera (L)
Young interviews the detective in charge of the case. Background of studio noise (L)	Varying shots of the detective, holding a shirt of the kind that was stolen, and the presenter (L)
Interview, with short VO by the detective, continues (L)	CCTV images showing the hijack of the lorry from an industrial estate (R)
Studio interview continues and concludes. Background of studio noise (L)	Shots of the detective and the presenter, followed by the presenter addressing the camera directly (L)
Presenter appeals for information about a murdered careworker (L). Music fades in (R)	Still photograph of murder victim (R)
Matthew trails an upcoming item (L) – about an African conman who emailed women with a promise of love and extracted large sums of money from them. Music bed continues (R)	Shot of Matthew in the studio, addressing camera (L)
Matthew's VO (L) followed by the remarks of one of the victims over the music bed (R)	Various images of postal workers sorting mail, emails, people sitting at computers and one of the victims addressing an unseen interviewer (R)
Matthew concludes the trailer (L)	Shot of Matthew in the studio, addressing camera (L)

Sounds	Images
Young introduces an item (L) about sexual assaults that have occurred in a student area of Manchester. Background of studio noise (L)	Shot of Young walking round the studio, addressing camera (L)
Dramatic music, traffic noises, voice of distraught young woman hailing cab driver, cab driver making 999 call (R)	Night-time shots of black cab driving down streets with a woman passenger in the back (R)
Music fades. DCI Mark Gibby narrates the outlines of the case (R)	Street shots, homing in on DCI Gibby, who is addressing the camera (R)
Dramatic music resumes, VO of one of the victims (R)	Shots of streets and of a young woman boarding, riding and alighting from a bus (R)
Gibby continues the narrative on a bed of street noises and music (R)	Gibby in the street, walking towards and past the camera (R)
Gibby's VO on music bed (R)	CCTV footage of the attacker walking along the road in which the assault occurred (R)
Woman's VO and sounds of the assault on a bed of music that builds to a climax (R)	Shots of narrator's silhouette intercut with reconstruction of the assault (R)
Gibby's narrative continues. Background of street noises (R)	Shot of Gibby in street, addressing camera (R)
Dialogue, woman narrator's VO, music bed (R)	Reconstruction of the assault continues, intercut with narrator's silhouette (R)
Gibby's VO takes up the account (R)	CCTV images of man fleeing after the assault (R)
Gibby continues the account (R)	Shot of Gibby in street, addressing camera (R)
Gibby's VO recounts another assault, dramatic music resumes, sounds of the assault (R)	Shots of woman walking in street and being violently assaulted, punctuated by a still drawing, presumably of the assailant (R)
Gibby continues the account on music bed (R)	Gibby in narrow alleyway, walking towards the camera (R)
Location sounds on music bed (R)	Shots of victim getting to her feet and staggering away (R)
VO of first victim resumes on music bed (R)	Further shots of victim intercut with silhouette of narrator (R)

Sounds	Images
Young interviews DCI Colin Larkin to glean further details of the case (L). Studio noises in background (L)	Presenter and detective talking in the studio (L), intercut with two artistic impressions of the assailant
Young introduces (L) some CCTV street footage of a possible witness to the incident	CCTV shots of man in street and the assailant fleeing along the opposite pavement (R)
Discussion between presenter and detective continues (L). Young introduces some more CCTV footage	Studio shot of presenter and detective (L)
Young and the detective talk over footage. Background of studio noise (L)	CCTV shots of the supposed assailant following another woman earlier on the night of the assault (R)
Studio discussion between Young and the detective continues (L)	Studio shot of presenter and detective (L)
Young concludes the item with an appeal to the viewers for further information, then introduces Rav and Matthew (L) with details of cases that viewers have assisted with	Presenter addressing the camera (L)
Rav introduces the case of murdered mother of two, Heather Barnett (L)	Rav addressing the camera (L)
Shouts and conversation of children. Dramatic music fades in (R)	Filmed reconstruction of the children's arrival home from school and discovery of their mother's body (R)
Rav announces that someone has been charged with the murder (L)	Rav addressing the camera (L)
Matthew introduces an item (L) about a mother and daughter who were killed by a fire in their home in Eastbourne	Matthew addressing the camera (L)
Dramatic music bed, shouts of children, sounds of fire (R)	Filmed reconstruction of the house fire, the victims and the arrival of the emergency services (R)
Matthew announces (L) that someone has been charged with both murders	Matthew addressing the camera (L)
Rav announces (L) that the discovery of a skeleton on a building site in Manchester has sparked a murder inquiry	Rav addressing the camera (L)

Sounds	Images
Dramatic music followed by the remarks of a forensic pathologist (R)	Shots of skeleton and pathology lab intercut with the pathologist addressing an unseen interviewer (R)
Remarks over music bed from a DCI connected with the case (R)	Pictures of the DCI talking to Rav in an office (R)
Rav announces (L) that progress has been made on the case, thanks to DNA profiling	Rav addressing the camera (L)
Matthew introduces (L) the case of a woman who was stabbed to death and left in the boot of her car	Matthew addressing the camera (L) followed by still photograph of victim (R)
Matthew announces (L) that a man has been convicted of her murder	Matthew addressing the camera (L) intercut with a still photograph of the killer (R)
Young introduces (L) an item about a young woman who was murdered in Porthmadog	Young addressing the camera in the studio (L) before a still photograph (R) of the victim
Young interviews the DI investigating the murder (L)	Camera pulls away to reveal the DI as well as Young and workers manning telephones in the studio (L)
DI explains that two items – tracksuit bottoms and a pair of trainers – were dumped a short distance from the woman's body (L)	Still photos of the two items (R)
Young's interview of the DI continues (L)	Studio shots of Young talking to the DI (L)
Young concludes the item (L) with an appeal for further information and introduces Rav with a second batch of 'wanted faces'	Young addressing the camera (L)
Rav describes each of the individuals who are wanted on various matters by the police (L). Background of studio noise (L)	Rav stands before a photogallery of people who are wanted by the police (L)
Young introduces an item (L) about 'lonely hearts' scams and cues a report by Matthew	Young walking through the studio addressing the camera (L)

Sounds	Images
On a music bed, the voices of investigators and victims (R)	Images of a letter-sorting office, banknotes, emails on a computer screen, talking heads (R)
Music continues under Matt's narrative VO (R) and soundtrack (R)	Shots of African street scenes, people writing emails, banknotes (R)
The reactions of a middle-aged woman victim (R)	Tearful woman addressing unseen interviewer (R)
Matthew's VO (R) on a bed of wistful music (R)	Shots of countryside and wedding photo of woman with her now deceased husband (R)
A sequence of the woman's remarks, sometimes as a VO (R), intercut with Matthew's VO (R), and both on the music bed (R)	Shots of woman addressing unseen interviewer, the woman typing at a computer, images of print on a computer screen. One still photograph of an American general whom her correspondent pretended to be (R)
Matthew's VO (R) continues the story. More dramatic music fades in (R)	Images of emails on a computer screen and bank statements (R)
Music bed continues. Woman explains why she parted with so much money to the man who corresponded with her (R)	Woman addressing unseen interviewer (R)
Matthew's and woman's VO on music bed (R)	Reconstruction of young African man writing emails. Images of banknotes (R)
Woman and Matthew continue the narrative on music bed (R)	Woman addressing unseen interviewer, intercut with a shot of her house (R)
Matthew's VO explains how the police intervened and exposed the scam before the woman could sell her house. Music continues (R)	Sequences of images of man whom scammer pretended to be (R)
Matthew's VO continues on music bed (R)	Shots of woman, the actor playing the fraudster, the London cityscape, a newspaper page, the offices of SOCA, the Serious Organised Crime Agency (R)
On a dramatic music bed, remarks of a senior manager at SOCA alternating with Matthew's VO (R)	Manager addressing unseen interviewer, intercut with images of websites and emails on computer screens, the female victim at her keyboard (R)

Sounds	Images
On a dramatic music bed, remarks of the manager at SOCA alternating with Matthew's VO (R)	Shots of manager intercut with the SOCA offices, a partially blacked-out photo of the Ghanaian businessman behind the scam, and a bank statement (R)
Matthew's VO (R) recounts a visit by SOCA officers to another supposed victim of the scam. Music bed yields to a background of traffic noise. The detective sergeant's remarks (R)	Images of a motorway and a car interior with the DS at the wheel (R)
Matthew's VO on bed of sound actuality (R)	Night-time shots of police officers calling at a house (R)
DS recounts the interview with the second victim (R). Dramatic music bed resumes (R)	Shots of street lights, then the DS back at the wheel of his car, intercut with images of banknotes (R)
Music bed continues under Matthew's VO, with concluding remarks from DS (R)	More images of emails on a computer screen and the Ghanaian fraudster, with concluding shots of the DS in his car (R)
Under a new music bed, Matthew's VO continues (R), with an inserted sound-bite from the manager at SOCA (R)	Images of the actor playing the fraudster at his keyboard and making written notes, still photos of attractive people whose identities the fraudsters steal (R)
Under a new music bed, Matthew's VO (R) reports that the fraudsters are located in Ghana. The narrative is then taken up by the SOCA manager (R)	Shots of a Ghanaian townscape, then of a postal sorting office with the SOCA manager examining sacks of mail (R)
Matthew's VO (R) reports that in order to identify the fraudsters, a *Crimewatch* undercover agent is posing as a wealthy businessman looking for love. Agent begins a conversation, interspersed with Matthew's explanations. Music bed continues (R)	Shots of the agent talking on the phone (R)
New music bed. Matthew's VO (R) recounts that the agent is flying to Ghana to meet the women he has been corresponding with. The rendezvous is to take place in a hotel lobby	Shots of Ghanaian street scenes, letters and photos from the agent's female correspondents, and finally the agent sitting in a hotel lobby which is being secretly filmed (R)

Sounds	Images
Dramatic music bed, conversation between agent and girl, intercut with VOs (R) from Matthew. The agent denounces the woman as a fraudster (R)	Still photo of the agent's first date, followed by arrival of a quite different-looking woman. Shots of their meeting, at the end of which she gets up and leaves (R)
Matthew's VO (R) on a bed of hotel sound actuality. Agent's remarks in response to a demand for money for a taxi journey. Agent reveals his identity and denounces the men (R). Matthew's VO continues on music soundtrack (R)	Still photo of the agent's second date, followed by the arrival of three men. At the end of the meeting the men leave and are arrested outside the hotel (R)
Matthew's VO reports the arrival of the third 'date' in the form of a man with a handgun. VO intercut with remarks from the SOCA manager. Music bed (R)	Shots of another man being arrested, police examining a handgun, the SOCA manager being interviewed and the suspects being questioned at the police station (R)
Matthew's VO concludes the story, at first on a bed of sound actuality and then on sombre music. Final soundbite from the first woman victim (R)	Shots of the arrest of the ringleader at his huge mansion in Ghana followed by rainy images of the woman's home in Britain and of the woman herself, weeping (R)
Discussion between Kirsty and Matthew (L) about the fraudsters' techniques and the sums of money they have extorted	Kirsty and Matthew facing each other in the studio (L)
Young concludes the item (L) and introduces Rav with a quick round-up of what's been happening on the phones tonight	Presenter addressing the camera (L)
Rav reports on the information received in relation to two of the cases the programme has featured. Rav then introduces a trail for the *Crimewatch Road Show* (L)	Presenter addressing the camera (L), intercut with various still photos (R) of the key people and objects in the cases
Female VO outlines the content of the show over dramatic music bed (R)	A sequence beginning and ending with the *Road Show* title and logo and including CCTV footage of a shop robbery and the perpetrators, shots of a Pink Floyd tribute band whose priceless guitar was stolen, and the reconstruction of a burglar breaking into a stately home (R)

Sounds	Images
Rav concludes the item (L)	Rav in the studio, addressing the camera (L)
Kirsty Young concludes the programme (L)	Young walking through the studio and addressing the camera (L)
Crimewatch theme music (R)	Programme credits roll under photos of 'wanted faces' and brief shots of escaping criminals and pursuing police vehicles (R)

- *A VO, probably R, accompanies a filmed trailer for* Imagine, *a BBC 1 arts programme tonight at 10.30 pm, which will feature violinist Nigel Kennedy*
- *A VO, probably L, accompanies a still photo as a reminder that this evening's episode of* EastEnders *is about to be repeated on BBC 3*
- *A trailer, with music and a VO (probably R), over filmed images of the comedy show* Mock the Week *(2005–), which returns on Thursday at 10.00 pm on BBC 2*
- *BBC 1 ident, with music soundtrack, of people flying kites (R). VO (L) introduces the* Ten o'Clock News *with Huw Edwards and Sharon Barbour*

10.00 pm NEWS, REGIONAL NEWS, WEATHER (L)

Sounds	Images
The long wait for the truth about the events of Bloody Sunday is over (L). Music bed: BBC News theme (R)	Newsreader in studio (L)
Newsreader's VO (L) on bed of location sounds and theme music (R)	Shots of today's rally in Londonderry and historic footage of the riots of 1972 (R)
The Prime Minister's reactions in the House of Commons to the findings of the Bloody Sunday inquiry (R). Music bed continues (R)	The Prime Minister at the Dispatch Box addressing the members of the House (R)
Newsreader's VO (L) on bed of location sounds, including the words of speakers addressing the crowds (R). Music bed continues (R)	Pictures of the rally in Londonderry, including three speakers who addressed the crowd (R)

Sounds	Images
Newsreader concludes the item and trails tonight's other big stories (L). Location sounds accompany each of the film clips (R). Music bed continues throughout (R)	Newsreader in the studio (L), followed by clips of American oil barons at an inquiry into the BP oil-spill; Rupert Murdoch; South African police at the World Cup (R)
Sharon Barbour trails the main stories in the North East (L). Music bed continues (R)	Newsreader in *Look North* studio (L)
Three more Cumbrian shooting victims are laid to rest. Some Cleveland Police staff are to be transferred to the private sector (L). Music bed continues throughout (R)	Clip of one of the funerals (R). Newsreader in *Look North* studio (L)
BBC News theme music swells to a conclusion (R)	Sequence of graphics of the world and the BBC logo (R)
Huw Edwards bids us good evening and outlines the findings of the Bloody Sunday inquiry (L). He cues a report from Allan Little, a special correspondent, in Derry	Newsreader standing in studio (L) with moving graphics and text (R) on a large screen behind him
Little's VO on a bed of location sounds (R)	Shots of today's rally in Londonderry (R)
Prime Minister's statement about the inquiry in the House of Commons intercut with applause from the crowd in Londonderry and Little's VO (R)	The Prime Minister at the Dispatch Box in the House of Commons intercut with pictures of the crowd in Londonderry (R)
Little continues his report (R)	Little addressing the camera from within the crowd at Londonderry (R)
Little's VO intercut with statements from some of the speakers at the rally (R)	More shots of the rally and of the speakers (R)
Little interviews two people who were directly affected by the events of Bloody Sunday, with a short VO between the two (R)	The interviewees being interviewed and addressing the rally (R)
Little's VO gives an account of the events of Bloody Sunday. Soundtrack of riots in the background (R)	Historic footage of Bloody Sunday riots, including pictures of the Republican Martin McGuinness. Sequence finishes with contemporary shots of McGuinness (R)

Sounds	Images
Martin McGuinness's reactions to the findings of the inquiry (R)	McGuinness making a statement in the street (R)
VO narrates that General Sir Mike Jackson, who later became head of the army, was a serving soldier in the Bloody Sunday riots (R)	Film of General Jackson as head of the army (R)
General Jackson's reaction to the findings of the inquiry (R)	Pictures of General Jackson reading a statement (R)
Little's VO observes that the inquiry opens the way to the prosecutions of a number of soldiers (R)	Aerial shots of today's rally in Londonderry (R)
Remarks by a member of the Democratic Unionist Party (R)	Shot of leader addressing an unseen interviewer (R)
Little's VO continues (R)	Still photographs of the victims of the Bloody Sunday shootings (R)
Little's VO concludes over the sounds of today's rally (R)	Shots of people at the rally bearing photos of the victims and being applauded by the crowd (R)
The newsreader reports (L) further remarks made by the Prime Minister and cues the defence correspondent Caroline Wyatt	Newsreader in the studio (L)
Wyatt's VO over the sounds of the 1972 riots (R)	More historic footage of the Bloody Sunday riots (R)
Colonel Stuart Tootal, a former paratroop commander, urges that the historical context of the army's actions should not be forgotten (R)	Tootal addressing an unseen interviewer (R)
Wyatt's VO continues over the soundtrack (R). Within it is inserted a brief condemnation of the soldiers' behaviour by a former army commander (R)	Resumption of 1972 footage of riots, encapsulating a shot of the army commander outside a public building (R)
Lawyer representing the criticised soldiers rejects the idea that the report could lead to prosecutions (R)	Lawyer addressing an unseen interviewer outside the Houses of Parliament (R)
Wyatt's VO (R) concludes the report	More historic footage, but with no soundtrack, of the riots (R)

Sounds	Images
Newsreader cues political correspondent Nick Robinson outside 10 Downing Street (L)	Shot of newsreader, then of both newsreader in studio and a screen image of Robinson at Downing Street (L)
Robinson delivers his report (L)	Robinson addressing the camera outside No. 10 (L)
Newsreader concludes the item, directing viewers who want further information to the BBC website (L)	Newsreader in the studio (L) followed by graphics and still images from the website (R)
Newsreader announces that three British soldiers have died in Afghanistan (L)	Newsreader addressing the camera (L) followed by moving graphic of map (R)
Newsreader introduces an item about the BP oil spill in the Gulf of Mexico. Oil executives have been subjected to congressional scrutiny (L). Mark Mardell reports	Newsreader addressing the camera (L)
Mardell's VO prefaces President Obama's remarks (R)	Shots of the President with US troops (R)
Mardell's VO continues over a bed of seaside sounds (R)	Shots of Gulf beaches (R)
Mardell's VO over a bed of the sounds of a senate committee hearing, intercut with some of the dialogue (R)	Footage of hearing (R)
Mardell's VO introduces concerns expressed by ordinary American holidaymakers, all on a bed of seaside sounds (R)	Footage of holidaymakers and Florida beaches (R)
Over sound actuality of the President being cheered by his troops, Mardell continues his report (R)	Shots of the President hailing the troops, with Mardell in the foreground, addressing the camera (R)
Newsreader announces (L) an upcoming item in the bulletin over a bed of the BBC News theme music (R). The music continues under the clip	Newsreader in the studio (L), followed by a clip of film director Oliver Stone with the President of Venezuela (R)
The theme music concludes as the newsreader introduces (L) the next item: Rupert Murdoch wishes to buy the rest of BSkyB. Business editor Robert Peston has the story	Newsreader addresses the camera (L). On the screen behind him a montage of images relating to BSkyB, some of them moving (R)

Sounds	Images
Peston opens his report as a VO (R)	Still photos of Rupert Murdoch and his son on a montage of images, some of them moving (R)
VO continues over faint film soundtrack (R)	Slo-mo images of Murdoch and his son
Peston continues his report (R)	Peston addressing the camera. Behind him a TV screen, showing statistics (R)
Peston's report continues as a VO (R)	Aerial footage of the BSkyB headquarters (R)
Remarks of Steve Hewlett, a media consultant (R)	Hewlett addressing an unseen interviewer (R)
Peston's VO continues (R)	More shots, external and internal, of BSkyB headquarters (R)
Remarks of Lib Dem MP Adrian Sanders (R)	Sanders addressing an unseen interviewer (R)
Peston's VO continues on a soundbed of the print workers' riots at Wapping in the mid-1980s (R)	Historic footage of the riots (R)
Soundtrack of advert launching Sky TV in 1989, Peston's VO continues (R)	Images of the advert. Brief image of Murdoch posing for photos (R)
Peston concludes his VO on the soundbed of the Sky montage (R)	Images of the web edition of the *Sunday Times* followed by montage of Sky-related images, over which the Sky logo fades in (R)
Newsreader announces (L) that President Chavez has marked Oliver Stone's new documentary about him by giving an interview to the BBC's Stephen Sackur	Newsreader addressing the camera (L), behind him a still photo of President Chavez of Venezuela (R)
Sackur's VO (R) on bed of location actuality including remarks by Oliver Stone and the President (R)	Shots of the activity at the premiere of Stone's documentary (R)
Sackur's interview with the President (R)	Film of the interview (R)
Sackur's VO on bed of location actuality (R)	Shots of President Chavez at the UN followed by Chavez with the President of Iran (R)
Continuation of Sackur's interview (R)	Film of the interview (R)

Sounds	Images
Sackur concludes his report over a bed of faint city noises (R)	Shots of Sackur against a view of the Venezuelan capital Caracas (R)
Newsreader announces (L) that stewards at the South African World Cup are going on strike over pay. Andrew Harding sends this report	Newsreader addressing the camera (L)
Harding's VO (R) followed by remarks from the demonstrators (R)	Footage of demonstrators confronted by the police and soldiers, individuals addressing an unseen interviewer (R)
Remarks from a local official of the World Cup Organising Committee (R)	The official talking at what appears to be a press conference (R)
Harding's VO continues (R)	Shots of a recent confrontation in Durban followed by pictures of local soccer fans (R)
Statement from an official of the National Union of Mineworkers intercut with a question from Harding (R)	The official addressing an off-camera Harding (R)
Harding concludes his report against a background of chanting protestors in Johannesburg (R)	Shots of the demonstrators pull away to reveal Harding addressing the camera (R)
Newsreader introduces the regional news programmes 'where you are' and bids us goodnight (L)	Newsreader in the studio, addressing the camera (L)
Theme music for the BBC North East regional news programme, *Look North* (R)	Moving image logo of BBC *Look North* news (R)
Newsreader Sharon Barbour leads (L) with the funerals of three of Derek Bird's victims. Alison Freeman reports from west Cumbria	Newsreader in the studio, addressing the camera (L)
Freeman opens her report (R)	Freeman addressing the camera in front of a local church (R)
Freeman's VO (R) on a background of location actuality and intercut with a remark from the local vicar (R)	Shots of one of the funerals, intercut with shot of vicar addressing an unseen interviewer (R)
Freeman reports on the second funeral, first as a direct address and then in a VO (R), all on a background of location actuality (R)	Brief shot of Freeman, then more funeral footage intercut with still photograph of the deceased (R)

Sounds	Images
Freeman concludes her report (R)	Freeman addressing the camera in front of a local church (R)
Newsreader introduces (L) an item about a soldier, newly returned from Afghanistan, who has been killed on a Teesside street. Latanya Shannon reports	Newsreader in studio, addressing the camera (L), large photograph of soldier in background (R)
Shannon's report delivered as a VO (R)	Photo of soldier fills screen, followed by shots of the murder scene in a Teesside street and a still photo of the soldier with his young family (R)
Newsreader announces that Cleveland Police will transfer several hundred of their administrative staff to a private company (L). Stuart Wincup reports	Newsreader in studio, addressing the camera (L)
Wincup's report delivered as a VO on a background of location sounds (R)	Footage of police making arrests in a city street followed by shots of administrative staff working in an office (R)
Remarks of an official from the trade union Unison (R)	Official addressing an unseen interviewer (R)
Wincup's report continues as a VO on bed of location sounds (R)	More shots of administrative staff working in an office (R)
Wincup continues his report on a background of location sounds (R)	Wincup addressing the camera from outside a police station whose wall is used as the background for the introduction of superimposed computer graphics, listing statistics (R)
Chair of Cleveland Police Authority's comments heard at first as a VO (R)	More shots of administrative staff (R)
Comments continue (R)	Chair of Police Authority addressing an unseen interviewer (R)
Wincup's report concludes as a VO (R)	Shots of police controlling crowds in the street (R)
Newsreader announces that researchers at Newcastle University have found a link between diet and lung cancer (L)	Newsreader in studio (L), bracketing shots of the university buildings and of people smoking cigarettes (R)
Newsreader cues the local weather forecast from Paul Mooney (L)	Newsreader in studio (L) with photo of seascape behind her (R)

Sounds	Images
Weather presenter delivers his forecast (L)	Forecaster (L) against a background of the weather logo, a still photograph, a map with moving graphics and a series of statistics (R)
Barbour concludes the bulletin (L), then the news theme music begins (R)	Newsreader in studio (L) followed by the moving image logo of BBC *Look North* news (R)
National weather presenter Rob McElwee delivers his forecast (L)	McElwee addressing the camera (L) in front of moving graphics, statistics, photos, animated maps (R)

- *A VO, probably L, trails the next programme, about the violinist Nigel Kennedy and accompanies a BBC 1 ident (R), advertising both* Imagine *and, later,* Crimewatch Update
- *A trailer, consisting mainly of a young woman talking to the camera over a music bed, for the BBC Radio 4 series* Material World *(R)*
- *A sequence of dramatic clips from the new drama season on BBC 1 (R)*
- *A BBC 1 ident of helicopter approaching a lighthouse, with engine noise and dramatic music (R). VO, probably L, trails* Crimewatch Update *later on, but first the* Imagine *series features musical maverick Nigel Kennedy*

10.35 pm IMAGINE (R)

The programme portrays the new life of violinist Nigel Kennedy at his home in southern Poland.

A number of other 'pasts' are combined with the past in which this programme was recorded. There are clips of Kennedy playing the violin as a child; as a youth; as a student at the Juilliard School; as a concert performer in his twenties.

There is also footage of Lech Walesa leading the Polish Solidarity movement in the 1980s.

- *A trailer of clips, music and a VO for* Gareth Malone Goes to Glyndebourne *on Thursday on BBC 2 (R)*
- *A trailer of clips, music and a VO for next Wednesday's* Lennon Naked, *part of the 'Fatherhood' season on BBC 4 (R)*
- *BBC 1 ident, with music soundtrack of people flying kites (R). VO (L) introduces* Crimewatch Update

11.25 pm CRIMEWATCH UPDATE (L)

Sounds	Images
Crimewatch theme music (R)	Sequence of images of a helicopter, police and forensic activity and fleeing criminals, concluding with the *Crimewatch* title (R)
Kirsty Young welcomes us back and begins with an update on the burglary in County Durham (L)	Young addressing the camera and walking through the studio (L)
Soundtrack of the dramatic reconstruction of the crime, intercut with the victim's own recollections, all on a bed of dramatic music (R)	Rerun of the dramatic reconstruction of the crime, intercut with victim addressing an unseen interviewer (R)
Presenter interviews the DI investigating the case, who gives an update (L)	Shots of the DI and the presenter (L) plus two still photos (R) of a car being sought in connection with the case
Matthew reminds us of the murder of Barry Rubery in Gloucestershire (L)	Camera pulls away from still photo of victim (R) to Matthew in the studio (L)
Matthew's VO (L?) on a bed of dramatic music and sounds of the attack on Rubery (R)	Rerun of the dramatic reconstruction of the crime (R)
Recollection of the victim's daughter on bed of mournful music (R)	Victim's daughter addressing unseen interviewer (R)
Matthew interviews the DI investigating the case, who gives an update (L)	Shots of the DI and Matthew (L), plus still photo (R) of type of Land Rover seen at the scene of the crime
Rav gives updates (L) on the crimes featured in the earlier programme that were captured on CCTV	Rav addressing the camera (L) alongside a screen showing still images of the wanted individuals (R)
Young reports updates on the sexual assaults on students in Manchester (L)	Presenter addressing the camera (L)
Victim's VO on bed of dramatic music, sounds of an assault, snatches of dialogue (R)	Rerun of the dramatic reconstruction of one of the crimes (R)
Young interviews the DI investigating the case, who gives an update (L)	Shots of the presenter and the DI (L) interspersed with still images of the suspected assailant (R)

Sounds	Images
Matthew interviews the DI investigating the murder of a young woman in Porthmadog (L)	Shots of Matthew and the DI (L) interspersed with still images of the trainers and tracksuit bottoms (R)
Rav gives updates on several of the 'wanted faces' (L)	Rav (L) standing in front of the gallery of 'wanted faces' (R)
Young gives update on the Ghanaian 'lonely hearts' scam and closes the programme (L)	Young walking through the studio and addressing the camera (L)
Crimewatch theme music plays out (R)	Travelling shots through the *Crimewatch* studio (L), with rolling credits (R)

- *The BBC 1 logo trailing* The Graham Norton Show *(2007–) (R), accompanied by a VO (L) telling us that the show is up next*
- *VO (L?) announces that the BBC Trust would like to gather audience views on Radio 3, Radio 4 or Radio 7. The screen shows contact details underneath the logos of the stations (R)*
- *Trailer advertising* Mongrels, *a puppet show for adults showing next Tuesday on BBC 3 (R)*
- *Trailer for tomorrow's World Cup match between Spain and Switzerland, live on BBC 1 (R)*
- *Over a moving logo of BBC, with music bed, a VO, probably L, introduces …*

11.35 pm THE GRAHAM NORTON SHOW (R)

Norton begins by announcing that although the World Cup is underway, the show is being recorded before England's first game. Since the date of this transmission is 15 June and England's first game took place on 12 June, the recording must be at least three days old.

Norton follows this by saying, ostensibly to the viewers as well as to the live audience, 'We've got a great show for you *tonight* [my emphasis]'. The guests, illustrated with still photos, are Amanda Holden, Bill Bailey and Kelly Rowland.

At one point in the programme there is what appears to be a live conversation on Skype between Norton and Johnny Jenkins, an expert in music 'riffing' located in New Mexico. Norton brings up Jenkins's image on the screen of a computer located behind him, which then fills the television screen. The assertion that the conversation is Skyped seems truthful: Norton's picture is in a small panel at the bottom corner of the frame; the main picture, of Jenkins, is of typically poor quality, with jerky movements appearing out of sync with the sound.

Later, Kelly Rowland sings the track 'Commander' from her latest album. She is miked and backed by four dancers, but no band is visible and the instruments and electronic effects, along with the vocal backing, seem to have been pre-recorded. Norton then asks Rowland if she has to do training in order to sing and dance simultaneously since it was, he avers, a 'live vocal'. The aim of her performance is evidently to combine the excitement of liveness (an effect assisted by the dancers) with pre-recorded sounds that match as closely as possible those of the manufactured album track.

The show ends at approximately 12.25 am.

If we look at the totality of the evening's output – nearly six and a half hours – we can see that far more of it is recorded than live. More than half of the programmes are ostensibly live, although we immediately encounter the problem of what constitutes 'a programme'. In the *Guardian* schedule for BBC 1 on this day, the regional news is listed as a separate programme at 6.30 pm but not at 10.25 pm, when it is treated merely as an appendage of the national news. Of the nine separate programmes it lists, we can say that five – the *6 o'Clock News and Weather*, the *Regional News*, *Crimewatch*, the *10 o'Clock News* and *Crimewatch Update* – are live: but in temporal terms only about 43 per cent of the total output is live – two hours forty-five minutes out of the six hours twenty-five minutes that comprise the evening's viewing.

Even this gives a flattering picture of the extent of liveness because it is quite clear that the nominally live programmes also contain much that is pre-recorded. Even in the news, which we think of as live programming *par excellence*, live content is in a minority. Quite aside from the argument we considered in Chapter 2 that because they have been written earlier even the newsreader's words are not strictly live, there is scarcely an item that is devoid of recorded material. Moreover, by implying that one programme follows hard on the heels of another, the *Guardian* schedule is misleading: there are interstices that are filled by continuity announcements and trailers, many of which are pre-recorded. One could go so far as to say that there are very few moments in television output that are live, pure and simple. (There seem to be more of them in radio, whose all-sound content is often less layered: in a phone-in or studio discussion, for instance, one might hear nothing but live voices for considerable lengths of time.)

What purposes does all this pre-recording serve? First, let us remind ourselves of what television is. It is a medium which sends sounds and moving images over distances to a large, dispersed and mostly domesticated audience but like all media, its role is shaped by certain constraints. If these sounds (mostly words) and images do not significantly add to the ordinary first-hand experience of its viewers, they will be unwilling to watch it. On the other hand, once they can be persuaded to watch, its mainly domesticated nature means that their use of it will be at once casual and voracious. The role of pre-recording is therefore to create as economically as possible a vast amount of material that they will wish to watch, and we noted in Chapter 4 how one of its consequences was a rapid growth in the number of serial programmes. From our chosen evening of viewing we can see two other benefits of pre-recording that support this overall aim of enhancing watchability. The first is to make television content more *aesthetic* – more pleasing to the eye. Live transmissions which use several cameras are instantaneously edited by the programme director, but a pre-recorded, stable body of material allows editing to a much higher standard. Footage that is redundant or uninteresting or technically inferior can be removed, and selections and combinations more thoughtfully created. There is also an opportunity to add extraneous effects such as background music.

Since fictional television is less time sensitive than news and current affairs it can often show the aesthetics of pre-recording to better effect, but the dramatic reconstructions of *Crimewatch* illustrate that we can also observe it in fictional television that has factual pretensions. The discernible difference between live and recorded pictures lies not, as in the old days, in technical quality but in production values: the composition of the camera shots, the editing and shaping of the material. As part of the re-enactment of a violent assault that ended in a murder we see, on a soundbed of wistful music, some beautiful establishing shots of the Gloucestershire village in which it took place. This aestheticisation seems almost to reduce life to fiction and prompts the interesting question as to whether it enhances or distracts from the documentary aims of the reconstruction.

From our evening of programmes we can see a second benefit that can be achieved by the artful editing that is so much easier in pre-recorded material: it can secure viewer loyalty to a network by muddying the boundaries between programmes. Pre-recording was, of course, a huge gift to commercial television: without it, advertising breaks between and within programmes would have been almost unimaginable. Adverts could not only be made in advance of broadcast but copied for diffusion through any number of commercial networks. This means that depending on the legislation that governs the screening of adverts, and quite apart from any other material they will be carrying, these networks will be transmitting anything from seven to eighteen minutes' worth of pre-recorded material in any one hour – between 11 and 30 per cent of total output.

The BBC is a non-commercial broadcaster, yet what are trailers and promos if not adverts? – and there are almost as many of these on its networks as there are conventional adverts on those of its competitors. What is interesting is the way they are deployed. The Regional News ends just before 7.00 pm and over a filmed BBC logo, a continuity voice, probably though not certainly live, announces the start of the soap opera *EastEnders*. Yet *EastEnders* is not what follows. Up next is a filmed trailer about the violinist Nigel Kennedy, the subject of the *Imagine* programme which will be screened later in the evening. This is followed by a recorded promo for the BBC's online coverage of the World Cup, another recorded promo for Radio 1 Live Music and then a recorded trailer for the sci-fi drama serial *Doctor Who*. Finally, over the introductory music and images of *EastEnders*, a voice, probably though not certainly live, trails the hospital soap opera *Holby City*, which is coming up in an hour's time.

Thanks largely to the flexibility afforded by pre-recording, there is no easy switch-off point in this sequence. The aim is to discourage viewers from turning to a rival channel, and it was first noted a long time ago (Williams, 1974, pp. 86–94; Ellis, 1982, pp. 117–19). But what is rather more recent is an intensity in the competition for audiences that forces the BBC to be as self-promoting as its rivals. Indeed, what is being promoted above all else is the network or 'brand'– not so much the individual programmes that the trailers proclaim, since their positioning frequently threatens the integrity of these programmes, as simply 'an evening's *viewing*' on BBC 1.

However, all these benefits come at a price – a loss of the liveness which we have omitted from our definition of television earlier in this chapter but which, as we noted in Chapter 1, is historically its key distinguishing feature. Without liveness radio and television would have offered nothing new, and while it is true that there are now TV channels that specialise in feature films, we could reasonably regard them as a domestic form of cinema rather than television. (We shall in any case have more to say later about these channels.) For this reason, pre-recorded material on the television constantly behaves as if it *is* live. Liveness is, in a memorable word, an 'ideological' principle of the medium (Gripsrud, 1998, p. 19), and our evening's viewing provides numerous examples of this live behaviour. In the 10.25 pm Regional News bulletin, Sharon Barbour opens an item about the funerals of three of Derek Bird's victims with the present-tense cue, 'Alison Freeman *reports* from west Cumbria'. Yet this is plainly not a live report: even those viewers who might have missed the pictures when they were first screened some four hours earlier will note that they were shot in daytime and not in the late evening when they are now being shown. To strengthen the illusion of liveness in *EastEnders* there are fleeting shots of bunting and posters celebrating England's current World Cup campaign.

Sometimes it is impossible to tell what is live and what is recorded. For many years now there has been no difference in picture quality between live images and film, so how are we able to distinguish them? Usually from circumstantial evidence, such as the fact that the images we are viewing on a winter's evening were shot in broad daylight with the trees in full leaf, or that there is a conversational reference to ongoing events which we know belong to the past. Sometimes we become aware that the programme we are watching is simply too well constructed to have been created live. But sometimes we cannot be sure. The 10.00 pm News includes a report on the events in Londonderry from Allan Little but, while the images are evidently recorded, it is not clear whether the VO that accompanies them is recorded or live. In *Crimewatch* one of the presenters, Matthew, gives two full reports – the first on a murder in a Gloucestershire village, the second about lonely-hearts fraudsters. When watching my own off-air recording of the programme, I decided that Matthew's VO in the first story was live and in the second was recorded, and with hindsight I am a little puzzled as to why I reached these differing decisions. It could only have been because they were in reality 'too close to call' and it is quite likely that I was wrong about both.

We might assume that continuity announcements are live because there is always a risk of breakdowns in transmission or interruptions to the schedule, and such unforeseeable occurrences therefore require *ad hoc* announcements. But the matter is complex. When waiting for a train at my local station I am always amused by the Tannoy announcements because their robotic, unlifelike inflections declare that they are pre-recorded. Yet since they always seem able to explain the cause of breakdowns and delays in the service, however various these might be, I am also impressed by their lifelike flexibility. My point, then, is that pre-recording can seem more spontaneous and adaptable than we might suppose.

The examples I have just cited illustrate a further point: that the relationship between liveness and recording is complex not simply because it can be hard to tell which is which but because it is one of *superimposition* as well as *juxtaposition*. In other words, liveness and recording do not simply alternate, with a wholly recorded sequence following a wholly live one and vice versa: they coexist. A live continuity announcement might be heard over a recorded network logo. The news-reader's live account of the Bloody Sunday inquiry is sometimes part of a message that simultaneously involves three different levels of record-ing: film of the rally in Londonderry, soundtrack of the rally in Londonderry and the BBC News theme music. In the above description of the news programmes I have sometimes noted that the newsreader or one of the presenters is positioned in front of a photograph. Since a photograph is a recorded image, this is a simple but easily overlooked instance of the interplay of liveness and recording.

A last but vivid instance of their complex relationship comes from *The Graham Norton Show*. One of Norton's guests, Kelly Rowland, appears (if we can so put it) to sing a track from her latest album. Although Rowland is miked, the viewer may doubt that this is a live performance because the sound seems far richer than those who are in vision could be expected to make. Apart from Rowland herself we can hear vocal backing, musical instruments and electronic effects, but no vocalists or musicians are in view – merely four dancers. There is, however, no admission that what we have heard is recorded: instead Norton asks Rowland if she needs to train for what is, he explains, a 'live vocal' during which she has to sing and dance at the same time. What we have just seen and heard, then, is a form of karaoke: a song sung live (the liveness suitably enhanced by all the dancing) over backing tracks that are pre-recorded. Yet even this isn't the whole of the matter. I have identified the respect in which Rowland is live, but this is only liveness *vis à vis* the studio audience: we should recall that the entire programme has been recorded and that the viewer is witnessing this 'live' perform-ance several days after it occurred.

But in television does recording always try to pass itself off as live-ness? At one point Graham Norton makes the relatively unusual admis-sion that his show is being pre-recorded. Given the abundance of old movies and vintage comedy shows on television, the illusion of contin-uous liveness is never completely sustainable: on this very evening, the news bulletins have been showing film of Bloody Sunday which is nearly forty years old. The illusion that Norton's show is live is much more plausible, yet he evidently felt it was worth suspending for the sake of a facetious prediction about England's performance in the World Cup (one that turned out to be horribly prescient). A moment later, however, the illusion is perhaps restored when he says 'We've got a great show for you *tonight*'. Does that 'tonight' refer to the night of the recording or the night of its broadcast? Possibly both, but almost certainly the latter.

When using the terms 'live' and 'recorded' we are in essence talking about a contrast between the present and the past and, given that in television the difference between the two is sometimes apparent and even affirmed, we also need to be aware that it frequently incorporates more than one past. Three or four examples from our evening's viewing show an interesting interplay between the 'present' of the programme, whether live or pre-recorded, and the several pasts that are located within it. The first is Caroline Wyatt's report in the 6.00 pm News on the reactions to the Bloody Sunday inquiry. The newsreader's introduction to it is of course live, but the whole of Wyatt's report is recorded. Within it, three different times are blended: there is the *very recent past* of Wyatt's own voiceover which packages the report; the *recent past* of those who are reacting to the report – Sir Mike Jackson, the lawyer Stephen Pollard and Colonel Stuart Tootal; and the *distant past* (1972) of the images and sounds of Bloody Sunday.

All we know for certain is that Wyatt's words are the most recent and the footage of Bloody Sunday is the oldest. We do not know in what sequence Jackson, Pollard and Tootal were recorded – possibly, though by no means certainly, in the sequence in which they appear. In television as in literature, a narrative unity is forged from a number of pasts that are blended in a way that transcends chronology. For viewing purposes – that is, in order for us to make the best sense of the reactions to the Bloody Sunday inquiry – the significant sequence is not the one in which these interviews and the Bloody Sunday fighting occurred but that of Wyatt's report and, according to the conventions of television, this is presented as if live.

It is worth glancing at three more items which combine different pasts. The *Imagine* programme about the violinist Nigel Kennedy is evidently pre-recorded, but within this recent recording, which focuses on Kennedy's present life in Poland, are older ones: Kennedy performing as a child; as a teenager; as a student at the Juilliard School; and some footage of the Polish Solidarity movement dating from the 1980s. However, the live show *Crimewatch* mingles not only different pasts but pasts of a different ontological status: live narrative might frame a recorded interview with the victim of a crime, shots of a fictional version of the victim in a reconstruction of the crime and CCTV footage of events happening near the scene of the crime and at about the time it was committed. There is the 'distant' past when the crime took place (evoked by the CCTV pictures) and the more recent pasts of the victim's recollection of it and a reconstructed version of it which in a sense belongs to the realm of make-believe.

The story about the attacks on female students in Manchester offers the best instance of this temporal complexity. Two victims are featured but the coverage of the first victim alone involves pre-recordings which were made at six different times, perhaps more, and which represent different kinds of reality. Kirsty Young's introduction and conclusion of the story are live, and near the end of it she also conducts a live interview with DCI Colin Larkin. But the pasts within it are: the time that the attack was reconstructed by *Crimewatch*; the time that the dramatic music bed was recorded; the time that DCI Gibby was filmed delivering his narrative on the streets of Manchester; the time that the victim gave her own reactions, partly in silhouette and partly as a VO; the time DCI Gibby recorded his VO; and the time, close to that of the attack itself, when CCTV footage caught the supposed attacker. Moreover, the dramatic reconstruction of the attack, which includes a fictional version of the victim, the image and words of the actual victim, the narration of DCI Gibby and the murky but real-life images of the CCTV cameras embody at least three different kinds of reality.

Our third item – about the new stage version of the old TV sitcom *Dad's Army* (1968–77) – comes from *Look North*, the early evening regional news programme. It opens with a live introduction from the newsreader on a bed of the sitcom's theme tune which was recorded by Bud Flanagan in 1968. There follows a reporter's recently recorded VO over a vintage excerpt from the television sitcom, then more recent footage of the stage version alternating with the television version. But the recency of the recording of the stage version is then merged into the present, and indeed the future, with the newsreader's concluding statement that 'the show runs until Saturday', in effect positioning the item as a live promo. It is thus possible to see the recorded elements within this item as the background to a currently running or 'live' phenomenon that has future implications (that is, 'you've still got time to go and see it').

The different kinds of recording in our evening's viewing therefore show us that there is more than one past, but the Skyping episode in *The Graham Norton Show* offers an oblique reminder that there is also more than one present. We established in Chapter 2 that a live encounter in the traditional sense was an encounter between people who shared a single time and space. When Norton Skypes Johnny Jenkins they are by definition in a single moment and place, yet the former is also in the United Kingdom, let us say at 9 o'clock on a cool, dark evening, while Jenkins is in New Mexico at 3 o'clock on a hot, sunny afternoon. It is true that this particular encounter provides no visible evidence of this, but it reminds us nonetheless of the quintessential achievement, the extraordinary paradox, of broadcasting. In Paddy Scannell's vivid phrase, broadcasting allows us 'new possibilities of being: of being in two places at once, or two times at once' (Scannell, 1996, p. 91). Of course, Skyping is not of itself broadcasting, and the achievement of both is shared by telephony, but it was broadcasting which increased the scale of such quasi-live encounters and first brought a visual dimension to them.

Since television provides more than one present and often more than one past, it can sometimes be helpful to replace the usual strict dichotomy of liveness/recording with something looser like 'contemporariness' on the one hand and a separate, more distant past on the other. The former would embrace both the actual present and the recent past and approximates to the 'zone of liveness' we talked about in Chapter 6. In the Regional News feature on *Dad's Army*, for instance, the snatches of the stage version are evidently pre-recorded, but since it is still running they could just as easily be live and in any case, the aim is to advise us that we can go along and see it until next Saturday. A similar contemporariness attaches to the items in the News and *Crimewatch*. Bloody Sunday occurred forty years ago, but how will the findings of the inquiry influence the political future of Ireland? The crimes of *Crimewatch* occurred at varying times in the past but their perpetrators are still at large, so can the programme lead to their arrest and conviction? 'Contemporariness' is, in effect, a means of squaring the circle. Its audience expects television to fulfil its historically unique ability to provide material that is live and, because the medium is domestic and easy to access, to do so in abundance. But since it is extremely hard to find an abundance of live material that is interesting, that which is more broadly contemporary will help to meet the demand with every appearance of liveness.

So when and why is real liveness declared on television? When will mere contemporariness – the 'zone of liveness' – no longer suffice? Despite the almost continuous pretence of liveness, viewers are well aware that much of what they see is pre-recorded. So when something happens that is time-sensitive, television must revert to its core competency and reaffirm its *literal* liveness, and there are at least two instances of this in our evening's viewing. The first comes at the end of the Bloody Sunday story in the early evening News, when from outside 10 Downing Street, political editor Nick Robinson assesses the likely impact of the official inquiry on the peace process in Northern Ireland. His liveness may be seen to perform two roles: first, it reminds us of the 'present-tense' nature of the story, the fact that the inquiry is something that does not simply seek to bring closure to the events of the past but will have an impact on the future; second, it symbolises how near the BBC is to the political epicentre of the story.

The second example of literal liveness comes from the early evening Regional News, a report on the privatisation of several hundred employees of Cleveland Police. Note the slight but significant difference between the way in which this story is cued – 'Stuart Wincup is in Middlesbrough for us now' – and another cue, 'Alison Freeman reports from west Cumbria', which opens a recorded item on the funerals of Derek Bird's victims. Unlike Freeman, Wincup is not merely *reporting* from the imprecisely defined location of the event, he is *existing* at it – and this spatial and temporal specificity is reinforced by that extra word 'now'. In fact, it is only Wincup's framing of the story that is live, but since all the others in the programme are wholly pre-recorded, his presence is a badge of its gravity. In this part of the country, where unemployment is endemic and the recession at its deepest, jobs and the economy are the main preoccupation, and if any updates or emendations to the story are needed, Wincup is at the scene.

We have not addressed all the paradoxes of liveness and recording in broadcasting, for it is a curious fact that, while its audiences expect its output to be live, they are often willing to record it off-air for consumption at a later date. But this is a topic for the next chapter.

8 Broadcasting and Time-shifted Consumption

If liveness is so crucial to broadcasting we must address not only the fact that broadcasters transmit a massive amount of material which has been pre-recorded but that viewers and listeners do not always consume it at the moment it is being transmitted. To put it another way: if broadcasting's historically unique quality is liveness, why do viewers and listeners spurn it by delaying their consumption of its output? The history of time-shifted consumption throws some interesting light on the idea of liveness, perhaps clarifying the limits of broadcasting by confirming that the less concerned the audience is with the temporal, or more precisely the temporary, the less like 'broadcasting' the output seems. In our discussion we will again focus on television, though much of what we argue will also be applicable to radio.

Until quite recently it was off-air recording technology which provided the main means of time-shifted consumption and, since it also admitted to television screens and radio loud-speakers all kinds of material that had not previously been broadcast, which made the biggest stride towards media convergence. As well as programmes that had been transmitted over the air, radio receivers could play commercial audio cassettes and home-made recordings, while TV sets could screen Hollywood-style feature films, commercial videos and home-made movies. In a word, radios doubled as record players or tape-recorders and televisions doubled as film projection screens or domestic cinemas.

The off-air recording of television programmes became possible in 1972 with the advent of the video-cassette recorder (VCR). Domestic sales were at first inhibited by the existence of several competing and incompatible formats, notably VHS and Sony Betamax, but VCRs soon incorporated a whole range of features – remote control, digital timing, fast forward and rewind, freeze-frame, slow-motion and speeded-up replay – and by 1986, had found a place in half the homes of the UK (Armes, 1988, p. 156). Their reign was ended only by the digital versatile disc (DVD) player, which became commercially available in Japan in 1996, the United States in 1997 and Europe in 1998. DVDs offered better picture and sound quality, easier access to selected parts of the recording and greater ease of use, storage and transport (Roberts, 2006, p. 31). But at the turn of the century, other modes of off-air recording appeared. From 1999, a 'personal video recorder' named TiVo could be used to build a profile of an individual viewer's tastes and automatically record what it thought she would like, and since 2001, Sky Plus has enabled viewers to record, pause and instantly review live television. These devices mean that time-delay can now be deployed to even greater effect in reception than in production (Marriott, 2007, p. 49). The users of Sky Plus can replay live television instantly, let us say for about five minutes, and then, if they wish, return to the live transmission; or they can simply 'stay with the replay' and continue for an indefinite period to watch television's content some five minutes after it has actually been transmitted.

The most recent means of time-shifted consumption involves the viewer in no off-air recording of any kind. This is the BBC iPlayer, which since 2007 has enabled audiences to consume the corporation's radio and television programmes for up to a week after they have been broadcast. Instead of being obliged to store them on a set-top box, the audiences can use computers and mobile phones to access them in the form of data which is streamed from the BBC's website.

Why do audiences watch or listen to programmes at times other than those during which they are transmitted? While obvious in themselves, the reasons have interesting implications that are worth exploring. First, viewers and listeners wish to consume at a time convenient to them the broadcast content they would otherwise miss. For broadcasters, time-shifted consumption makes the scheduling of programmes a somewhat less crucial matter, at least in respect of some genres. (The two evident exceptions are the news, which audiences will wish to consume live, and programmes with 'adult' content.) Nevertheless, within the vast corpus of programmes that audiences might wish to time-shift, some material can be caught up with at any time while other material is time sensitive and must be consumed as-live within that 'zone of liveness' or period of contemporariness that we identified in Chapter 6. For reasons that are clear, the difference roughly corresponds to the difference between fictional and factual programmes – but only roughly.

What is interesting is the extent to which the delayed consumption of time-sensitive material *aspires* to liveness, or is at least permeated by a sense of topicality. As we noted in Chapter 6, it is not so much a question of the viewer (or listener) wanting to catch up with what she has recently missed as imagining that the programme is being transmitted in the here and now. It has been shrewdly observed that such viewing detaches the viewer's personal experience of 'live' television from the actual transmission of the live broadcast (Lury, 2005, p. 110) and this experience is helped by the fact that consuming the iconic media of theatre, cinema, television and radio is always, in a sense, a 'present-tense' activity: unlike words, sounds and images cannot express the past. In these iconic media there are, of course, often reminders that the content does belong to the past, such as the inferior technical quality of the recording, the archaic speech and accents of the actors, the dated styles of dress, and the allusions to contemporary affairs that are now history. But none of these factors mitigate the sense of liveness in the viewer's consumption of material that has been recorded very recently.

Her desire that broadcast content should be for the most part live, or failing that, as near live as can be, is borne out by some recent statistics. First, even among Sky viewers, 83 per cent of viewing remains live: only 17 per cent is time-shifted, and time-shifting accounts for a mere 6 per cent of all viewing. Second, more than half of all time-shifted viewing takes place *within a day of the original transmission*, apparently because people wish to share their reactions to it (Pennington, 2010, p. 4). This kind of time-shifting thus focuses attention on what 'live' television actually means (Lury, 2005, p. 111): it is not simply about the individual experience of the viewer but bound up with *simultaneity* of consumption, with the viewer's awareness during the live transmission that countless other viewers are watching at the same time.

The second reason for time-shifted consumption is to allow repeat viewing: to help the viewer to better understand and appreciate the programmes she has already seen. In this role, it provides a somewhat disconcerting reminder of the potential *inadequacy* of liveness, of our frequent inability to assimilate in a single act of consumption material that exists in a time-based, evanescent medium. Much depends, of course, on the nature of this material, but on occasions television, when consumed live, can seem to be unequal to the complexity of the content it seeks to convey. Certain pre-scripted programmes, most obviously dramas, contain more complications and allusions – twists in the plot, explanations for certain actions and events, interactions between characters – than many of us can absorb in a single viewing. Even the narrative of an historical or scientific documentary can be hard for us to follow. On a strict analysis, does this mean that television – broadcasting – has always provided material which is to a notable extent beyond the comprehension of its audience? Even if that is so, the fact that much of this material is now reviewable seems to be influencing the way in which scriptwriters are approaching it:

> Much of the best television is not watched on television, but on DVD and via internet downloads. A new confidence that audiences will use technology to keep track of complex plotlines has fed a rebirth of dramatic nuance, writers say ...
>
> (Blakely, 2011, p. 45)

We ought finally to notice that the older time-shifting technologies afforded a gratification to the audience that the newer technologies do not: they turned programmes into detachable artefacts that viewers and listeners could *possess* and *retain*. Just as pre-recording had meant tradeable goods for broadcasters, off-air recording in the guise of video cassettes and DVDs meant ownable goods for audiences (Crisell, 2002, pp. 216–17). Yet what is interesting is how the newer technologies have once again reduced the artefactual status of programmes by turning them back into ephemera: they have made the ownership of content not only slightly more difficult but conceivably less desirable. Following video cassettes and DVDs, TiVo and Sky Plus store off-air content inside a box – to be specific, on a hard disc: programmes are no longer retained by the viewer in a detachable piece of hardware. Moreover, because the disc is of relatively limited capacity the viewer frequently has to wipe what she has accumulated in order to make way for fresh material.

The great innovation of the BBC iPlayer is that it does not permit retention of any kind. Content which was recorded by the broadcaster at or before the time of transmission is streamed to the viewer or listener at a time to suit the latter: it is not content that has been captured within the receiving equipment she possesses. One could therefore describe the iPlayer as an instrument of both live broadcasting and deferred consumption: in the form of internet streaming, it is re-broadcasting that has been initiated by the viewer or listener. Moreover the content must always be consumed within the zone of liveness or broad contemporariness that we have more than once described. Hence the iPlayer, and to some extent TiVo and Sky Plus, evoke a certain quality of liveness that is absent even from the taped and disc recordings of time-sensitive material like *Match of the Day*: you only have so long in which to watch or hear the content – and you don't have the option of keeping it. After the era of video cassettes and DVDs, then, these more recent devices strike a renewed blow for liveness by evoking the precious impermanence of live output. We have mentioned one quality of broadcast liveness: the sense of commonality or community that it creates – a consciousness in each viewer that many other viewers are watching at the same moment. Another quality, inherent in all kinds of liveness, is that it cannot in any absolute or comprehensive sense be possessed. It is like sand: the harder you grasp it, the more it slips through your fingers.

The ownership of programmes is still, of course, an option. VCRs and DVD recorders remain widespread, and one can buy DVDs from stores that sell not only cinema films (many of them subsequently screened by television) but classic television series. Nevertheless the newer technologies are perhaps the beginning of a trend to separate the time-shifted consumption of broadcast content from the ownership of it and to make the consumer pay separately for the latter. Yet it is also true that the purchase of DVDs is less popular than the cheaper option of rental: sales of the former have been falling since 2007, and according to one account went into a steep dive – 19 per cent – in the first quarter of 2011 (Sabbagh, 2011, p. 27). However, *mailed* DVD rental is also in decline: what is offsetting both is *on-line* rental – the streaming of content to home computers, in return for a monthly subscription, by companies like Netflix and LOVEFiLM. Even though it is content that the subscribers do not get to keep, the future seems to lie with the download and not with the DVD.

While the sales of both cinema films and TV programmes are declining, it is just possible that the causes are somewhat different. At the time of writing, the mainstream film industry is in something of a trough: for both scriptwriters and well-known actors the long-form television dramas so successfully generated by Home Box Office are a more attractive prospect, so Hollywood has fallen back on formulaic series like *Pirates of the Caribbean* (2003–), which guarantee success but for the most part according to a law of gradually diminishing returns. These films are good enough to watch in a cinema and even to watch again on the television, but for many people perhaps not good enough to purchase outright. Moreover, the fact that so many of them are eventually seen on television perhaps helps to reposition them in the mind of the audience as part of television's run-of-the-mill content.

Why, then, are the DVD sales of television programmes also in decline? Again, it is just possible that potential purchasers are in some strange, half-conscious way inhibited by a sense that the medium is meant to be live. Television transmits each and every day, round the clock and on a multitude of channels: it simply generates too many programmes for more than a few to be permanently retainable. Perhaps viewers have an atavistic sense that broadcasting's artefacts are not only transient but *meant* to be so, that they must disappear in order to make way for their successors, and that this transience is part of the inherently live character for which we prize it.

We saw in Chapter 4 that recording, often serial recording, is used, paradoxically, to maintain a sense of liveness by helping to fill television's schedules day after day. On the other hand, significant numbers of the audience may be so imbued with a sense of its *actual* liveness as to wish not to retain its products. Despite the abundance of pre-recorded material and the ubiquity of time-shifted consumption, the enigma of liveness still confronts us.

Conclusion: Liveness, Recording, Broadcasting

The reader may feel that we are reaching the end of a book whose argument has been based on dubious premises. We began by suggesting that one way in which we might define broadcasting was in terms of the domestic or private nature of its consumption, but then we dismissed it not only because certain other media are similarly consumed but because a degree of public viewing and listening persists to this day. We asserted that liveness remained a better criterion. Yet we have seen that not all broadcasting is live: indeed, probably the greater part of it is not, and this is true even of ostensibly live programmes like the news. Moreover, a considerable amount of programming, whether live or not, is consumed some time after it has been transmitted. So why is liveness any more useful a way of defining broadcasting than domestication or privatisation?

The answer is that even though much of its content may be pre-recorded or consumed later than it is broadcast, the *transmission* of it is live: sending and receiving occur in the same instant. Entire television and radio channels may consist of recorded content – round-the-clock broadcasts of cinema feature films or 'robo-jock' music shows – but such content exists, so to speak, within a live envelope:

> [Broadcasting's] sense of liveness does not depend solely upon its programmes: it also lies in the very organisation of transmission. Transmission is live, even when the programmes are not. So recorded programmes are able to claim the status of liveness for themselves simply because the act of transmission attaches them to a particular moment.
>
> (Ellis, 2002, p. 31)

In a word, the *medium* or *contact* is live, even if the *message* or *content* is not. Moreover, the liveness of the transmission allows pre-recorded output to be replaced at any time by live output. If the wholly pre-recorded programmes of our radio or television channel should fail, a continuity announcer is able to make a verbal intervention or a duty engineer a technical one: 'liveness perpetually underpins the flow of broadcasting, always available as an option because the instantaneity of transmission and reception renders it a constant possibility' (Marriott, 2007, p. 58).

This being so, why does broadcasting typically pretend that its *programmes* as well as its transmissions are live – a pretence it drops only in respect of such blatant pre-recordings as Hollywood movies or vintage comedy shows? We noted in Chapter 7 that on a typical evening nearly 60 per cent of BBC 1's output was not live, and that when allowance was made for the pre-recorded inserts in the programmes that were ostensibly live, even this was a conservative estimate. As one scholar observes, 'Programmes adopt the rhetoric of liveness without being literally live' (Ellis, 2002, p. 33). I have put it more bluntly: broadcasting uses pre-recording 'with such a bad conscience that it disguises the fact' (Crisell, 2006, p. 160). The pretence is perhaps strongest in time-sensitive, topical shows like *Match of the Day*, which we looked at in Chapter 6.

Though programmes will sometimes talk about themselves as live when it is clear that they are not, the pretence of liveness is for the most part implicit in the conventions that broadcasting has adopted. One is the habitual use of the present tense to express things that have occurred in a pre-recorded past, and another is direct address, a feature that many scholars have noted in respect of television (e.g., Abercrombie, 1996, pp. 11–12, 18; Bourdon, 2000, p. 533; Ellis, 2002, p. 31; Marriott, 2007, p. 43). Direct address can, of course, be as easily recorded as any other form of television (or radio), so how does it evoke liveness? By simulating the face-to-face, unmediated mode of human communication which we characterised in Chapters 2 and 3 as the prototype of all others. With occasional help from an autocue, the speaker appears to look the viewer in the eye, a posture which seems to anticipate an instantaneous response from her and thus implies co-presence. Direct address is only rarely seen in the cinema, which like theatre adopts the convention that no addressee, in the sense of an audience, is present.

It is important to recognise the extent to which broadcasting's audience is willing to connive in the pretence of liveness. Whether or not its programmes are live, television is always sensed as live by the viewers (Altman, 1986, p. 45). As we saw in the last chapter, this is to some extent true of any medium that deals in images or sounds because these cannot of themselves express the past in the way that words can, so something that is taking place before our eyes and ears is something experienced in the present. Its future is ostensibly unknowable: we haven't, perhaps, seen or heard it before – and even if we have, so embedded in time are we that we act as if we haven't by anticipating other outcomes. On the other hand, we are aware that the pretence of liveness is sometimes unsustainable. In a shrewd analysis of the television show *Blind Date* (1999–2007), John Ellis (2002, pp. 34–5) shows how the events which have occurred between the contestants' first date and their reappearance on the show could not have taken place within the brief time scale that is claimed for them. It is perhaps this level of pretence which lies behind one scholar's observation that the less live television is, the more it insists it is (Feuer, 1983, p. 15).

Pre-recorded content is now so widespread in broadcasting and the pretence that it is live often so threadbare, that one BBC network feels it can derive a competitive advantage by incorporating liveness into its title: Radio 5 *Live*. In fact, the transmission of so much pre-recorded content is both live and non-live in the same way as are our examples in Chapter 2 of the envoy's message to the monarch, the newsreader's bulletin, the scholar's lecture and the enacted play. In each case the receiver or audience is part of a live communication in the sense that it receives the message at the instant it is delivered. Yet in the sense that all these messages were largely created earlier and elsewhere, those who are delivering them are merely their media, and the communication is not live. (To avoid confusion we might add that it is quite possible, indeed common, for media to exist within other media in the manner of Chinese boxes. Our newsreader is the medium for the news copy that a production journalist has written, but she also exists and functions within a much more elaborate and technological medium: television.)

However, in broadcasting as in other modes of communication, it can be only too easy to confuse the contact and the content, the medium and the message. Because in our prototypical, spoken and face-to-face mode the speaker delivers her own words directly to the listener and is thus the medium of her own message, the harbinger of bad tidings can sometimes be mistaken, and ill used, for being the author of them: he is then forced to plead 'Don't shoot me – I'm only the messenger!'. Likewise, because broadcasting is universally known to be a live, instantaneous medium, its often pre-recorded programmes may be mistaken for live ones – as we have seen, with the connivance of the broadcasters themselves.

In summary, then, the affirmation of liveness in television and radio is at one level unnecessary and at another largely untrue. It is unnecessary because it is self-evidently true of the *medium*: all broadcasting can be received at the instant it is transmitted. And it is untrue (and often unconvincing) because, although the pretence of liveness is maintained in nearly all of their programmes, we know that the great majority of them are pre-recorded. Why, then, do broadcasters persist with it? For much the same reason that the Kantian philosopher, whom we quoted in Chapter 3, pretends to be live – to be talking directly to someone rather than writing to an absent and invisible audience. Writing stands in the same relation to speech as recording stands to liveness, for both crave the human contact that they lack.

Let us remind ourselves of what is desirable about liveness. While 'live' and '*a*live' can mean much the same thing – 'animate', 'living', 'not dead' – we have been using 'live' mainly to describe an instantaneous *connection* between two things, leaving 'alive' to refer to the animate *state* that one or both of these things is in. Nevertheless there is little point in our having a *live* connection to something that is *lifeless* – in, for instance, being able to view a live image of a teaspoon. We desire a connection with things that manifest their existence in time, notably through movement and/or sound. Not all such things are alive but might still be of sufficient, if limited, interest for us to observe by means of a live connection: a working windmill or a seascape, for instance. (In the early days of television, the larger gaps between programmes were filled with just such images, known as 'interludes'. It is unlikely that they were live, but like all recorded material on television they had to have the semblance of liveness, be watchable enough to be live.) Yet what we require from liveness above all is a connection with the *living*, with the animal world in its broadest sense and essentially with our fellow humans, if not for their own sake then for every other aspect of existence as filtered through human intelligence. (To keep matters simple I have been discussing liveness in terms of images, but we should not ignore the significance of sounds. If our live image of the teaspoon were, for instance, accompanied by a voiceover explaining its history, aesthetic qualities, market value and so on, this would make it much more watchable.)

While connections to what is not alive may or may not be live, then, it is clear that the connections we crave with the living must be live, for if they are not live we cannot be sure that the living are not dead! And we crave these connections because life is on the whole preferable to its antitheses (recording, art, inertia, death) and is the yardstick against which we measure them. Whether or not life is eternal, as the Gospel of St John proclaims ('I am the Resurrection and the Life', ch. 11, v. 25), it is a universally desirable condition.

Since an inherent feature of life is its existence in time, the live media of theatre and broadcasting must also be time based. Liveness is precious, to be savoured, because each of its moments is both unique and transient: so what has been affirmed of theatrical performance – that it cannot be captured or recovered and indeed 'becomes itself through disappearance' (Phelan, 1993, p. 146) – is equally true of broadcasting's live representation of events in the real world. What it conveys seems honest and authentic and thrives on the spontaneous and unexpected (Bourdon, 2000, p. 537).

The disadvantages of liveness are simply its advantages turned inside out. For instance, the transience which makes it so precious renders it from another perspective worthless, endlessly wasting. For this reason, it has been suggested that the live or 'present-tense' medium of television (and by implication radio) lacks the definitiveness of a past-tense medium like writing or print and is therefore less authoritative (Lury, 2005, p. 123). Liveness is eternally inchoate – incomplete because it is always becoming something else. It is also potentially at odds with the prevailing tendency in media towards *audience autonomy*. A recent slogan of the European Broadcasting Union – 'Availability: anything, anytime, anywhere' – neatly expresses the wished-for shift in the balance of power between audiences and broadcast content. Audiences should no longer have to wait on 'events', whether in the form of content which the broadcasters have created or content which originates in the outside world. Wherever the audiences are and whatever the time, this content should be accessible, and so in order to make this happen liveness must in some sense be conquered or cheated.

It could be argued, however, that, thanks to rolling news channels, the events of the outside world can indeed be accessed both live and at any time to suit the audience: but aside from the fact that the concern of the slogan is with technological rather than scheduling solutions, even this is not strictly true. Such is the 'tyranny of the moment' that one must catch it when it occurs. If a viewer or listener turns to an all-news channel for live coverage of a particular event, she may still have to wait for it to come up within the ten- or fifteen-minute cycle of items that such channels typically operate. A much better way of combining up-to-dateness with audience autonomy is the stable, visual text of a constantly updated website: yet it is not live. If the audience craves live content it must surrender its autonomy to the moment in all its dominance and unpredictability. Hence, it is possible that as audience autonomy develops, broadcasting's essential liveness will paradoxically assume more significance, a point we will return to shortly.

The obvious rationale of recording is that it counteracts the fugitive, wasting nature of liveness by capturing broadcast content. We are already familiar with its logistical benefits: programmes, often of a serial nature, can be created and stockpiled before transmission and so help to supply the round-the-clock demand for content. They can also be turned into goods which can be exchanged between broadcasters, sold to audiences and consumed by the latter at times to suit themselves. Recording is, in short, an empowering tool for both the makers and consumers of programmes. But it brings other benefits. One is that it furnishes valuable historical evidence, whether about the state of broadcasting at a particular time or the state of the society it was serving. Another is that it confers a permanence on the products of radio and television which is the precondition of those art forms that are accorded the highest status. Thanks to their existence in stable media, painting, sculpture, literature and musical composition have over the centuries attracted much more attention and acclaim than the time-based art forms of dance, acting and musical performance because they were 'immortal' in a way that the latter were not. Consequently the reputations of painters, sculptors, poets, novelists and composers have been much more enduring than, for instance, those of actors, singers and musicians, for until recently the work of these individuals left no trace. We may learn, for instance, that one of the best-known artistic figures of the eighteenth century, David Garrick, was a brilliant actor who could do hilarious imitations of his former teacher Samuel Johnson. Of his brilliance and hilarity, however, nothing remains, whereas we can still read the poetry and essays of Johnson and so understand why his contemporaries (and subsequent generations) valued him so highly. Our greatest writer, William Shakespeare, was of course a dramatist: but because until recently that other key element of dramatic production – the performances of the actors – was short-lived, his work has traditionally been exalted as *literature* rather than drama.

All this changed with the arrival of recording technology, which stabilises – transfers to a spatial medium – activities and phenomena that originally existed in time, and though there may be theoretical debates about the way in which it should be determined (Ellis, 2005), we are now able to speak of a 'canon' of television and radio programmes, mostly, as we might expect, in the fields of drama, light entertainment and documentary. It is thus possible to see a paradox at the heart of broadcasting. On the one hand, it is a medium that is dedicated to ephemera – in a material sense even more so than the daily newspapers since its content 'vanishes', whereas the latter, once outdated, form a physical accumulation which must be burned, recycled or turned into fish-and-chip wrappers. Yet, on the other hand, some of its ephemera are sufficiently prized to be thought worthy of retention.

Recording nevertheless has its own limitations. In the service of art, research or mere sentimentalism, it provides a bulwark against the profligacy, the wastingness of life. It cheats the laws of time: ageing, the seasons, decay and death. It is immortal. Yet it preserves only by killing: sometimes in spite of appearances to the contrary, its contents are lifeless, inert. This conundrum – the eternal conflict between Life and Art (which we can see as 'recording' for the most valuable purposes) – has fascinated thinkers and writers throughout history, and perhaps found its most famous expression in Keats's 'Ode on a Grecian Urn'. The poet contemplates a Greek vase with its images of a musician playing pipes, a youthful singer and a lover with his girl underneath some leafy trees:

> Heard melodies are sweet, but those unheard
> Are sweeter, therefore ye soft pipes, play on;
> Not to the sensual ear, but, more endeared,
> Pipe to the spirit ditties of no tone.
> Fair youth, beneath the trees, thou canst not leave
> Thy song, nor ever can those trees be bare;
> Bold Lover, never, never canst thou kiss,
> Though winning near the goal – yet, do not grieve;
> She cannot fade, though thou hast not thy bliss,
> For ever wilt thou love, and she be fair!

Recording is a form of salvage – worth something, perhaps a great deal, but nevertheless 'defective', insufficient. Moreover, the media and content of recordings are themselves vulnerable to the effects of time. Keats's Grecian urn seems to have avoided damage to the extent that it is still recognisable and a thing of beauty, but films deteriorate with age and reflect worlds that are irretrievably bygone: because of changes in pronunciation and the cultural context, Shakespeare's word-play and allusions have become all but incomprehensible; sculptures are eroded by air pollution. When all allowances have been made for this fact, we may still feel that visual and sound recording retains many more of the trappings of liveness than writing and printing, those earlier forms of capture. It resembles the things it represents but, unlike paintings, statues and photographs, it also reflects their existence in time. Its dynamic character seems to restore the things to life, almost to defy the barriers between life and death or life and art. Through visual and sound recording, we can relive those agonising moments before the hijacked airliners crashed into the towers of the World Trade Center, moments when all was still intact and lives not yet lost, when we still feel we can wish it otherwise or at least savour the innocence before such harm was done. But the protagonists are as trapped as the characters on Keats's Grecian urn.

How can we expect liveness and recording to inform broadcasting in the future? We will be thinking primarily of television, though as always much of what we say will also apply to radio. To have a clear idea of the essential character of broadcasting, we should first ask some historical questions. Did it lose its distinctiveness, merge into something else, when it began to make use of pre-recorded content? Or when its audiences began to consume its content some time after they had received it? Or when television and radio sets began to provide material that had never been broadcast? Or when broadcast content began to be received not only on television and radio sets but on computers, laptops and mobile phones? In this book we have sought to characterise broadcasting not in terms of the ontological status of its content or the way in which its audiences have consumed it, or according to the apparatus by which it is received or which it shares with other media, but simply as the transmission of content to mass audiences, which, even if pre-recorded and/or consumed belatedly, is received instantaneously.

In itself, this feature means that whatever we are watching or listening to we tend to think of broadcasting as live, just as we tend to think of writing as speaking. In order to meet the insatiable demand for what is predominantly a domestic medium, broadcasting has always, and increasingly, carried material that is pre-recorded. However, now that there are other sources of pre-recorded content such as YouTube and LOVEFiLM, it is possible that broadcasting will gradually revert to something like its core competency. This would not exactly be the transmission of all-live material to an instantaneously viewing audience, for we have already noticed that even ostensibly live programmes like the news contain much material that has been recorded, but it could be material that is time sensitive – within what we have variously described as a zone of liveness or topicality. In a word, it may be that in future television and radio will focus much more on current affairs and sport. Television may also feature reality shows that solicit audience participation, while radio, as we noted in Chapter 5, may revive its love affair with live music. Yet despite the portents, we media students as much as anybody should heed the warning of the French playwright, Eugène Ionesco: 'You can only predict things after they've happened'.

Bibliography

Abercrombie, N. (1996) *Television and Society* (Cambridge: Polity Press).

Altman, R. (1986) 'Television/Sound', in T. Modleski (ed.) *Studies in Entertainment: Critical Approaches to Mass Culture* (Bloomington: Indiana University Press).

Armes, R. (1988) *On Video* (London and New York: Routledge).

Auslander, P. (1999) *Liveness: Performance in a Mediatized Culture* (London and New York: Routledge).

Bakewell, J. and N. Garnham (1970) *The New Priesthood: British Television Today* (Harmondsworth: Allen Lane/Penguin).

Barnard, S. (1989) *On the Air: Music Radio in Britain* (Milton Keynes: Open University Press).

—— (2000) *Studying Radio* (London: Arnold).

Blackburn, T. (2007) *Poptastic: My Life in Radio* (London: Cassell).

Blakely, R. (2011) 'Triumph of the TV: A Real-life Drama That Is Shaking Hollywood', *The Times*, 28 May.

Bourdon, J. (2000) 'Live Television Is Still Alive: On Television as an Unfulfilled Promise', *Media, Culture and Society* vol. 22 no. 5, pp. 531–56.

Briggs, A. (1970) *The History of Broadcasting in the United Kingdom: Volume III – The War of Words* (London: Oxford University Press).

—— (1995) *The History of Broadcasting in the United Kingdom: Volume V – Competition* (Oxford: Oxford University Press).

Caughie, J. (1991) 'Before the Golden Age: Early Television Drama', in J. Corner (ed.) *Popular Television in Britain* (London: BFI).

—— (2000) *Television Drama: Realism, Modernism and British Culture* (Oxford: Oxford University Press).

Chapman, J. (2005) *Comparative Media History* (Cambridge: Polity Press).

Chignell, H. (2009) *Key Concepts in Radio Studies* (London: Sage Publications).

Cooke, L. (2003) *British Television Drama: A History* (London: BFI).

Crisell, A. (1994) *Understanding Radio* (2nd edn) (London and New York: Routledge).

—— (2002) *An Introductory History of British Broadcasting* (2nd edn) (London and New York: Routledge).

—— (2006) *A Study of Modern Television: Thinking inside the Box* (Basingstoke: Palgrave Macmillan).

Ellis, J. (1982) *Visible Fictions* (London: Routledge and Kegan Paul).

—— (2002) *Seeing Things: Television in the Age of Uncertainty* (London: I. B. Tauris).

—— (2005) 'Importance, Significance, Cost and Value: Is an ITV Canon Possible?', in C. Johnson and R. Turnock (eds) *ITV Cultures: Independent Television over Fifty Years* (Maidenhead: Open University Press).

Feuer, J. (1983) 'The Concept of Live Television: Ontology as Ideology', in E. Kaplan (ed.) *Regarding Television: Critical Approaches – An Anthology* (Los Angeles, CA: American Film Institute).

Flew, T. (2007) *Understanding Global Media* (Basingstoke: Palgrave Macmillan).

Gifford, D. (1985) *The Golden Age of Radio* (London: Batsford).

Gripsrud, J. (1998) 'Television, Broadcasting, Flow: Key Metaphors in TV Theory', in C. Geraghty and D. Lusted (eds) *The Television Studies Book* (London: Edward Arnold).

Harvey, S. (2002) 'Making Media Policy', in A. Briggs and P. Cobley (eds) *The Media: An Introduction* (2nd edn) (Harlow: Longman).

Hesmondhalgh, D. (2002) *The Cultural Industries* (London: Sage Publications).

Jacobs, J. (2000) *The Intimate Screen: Early British Television Drama* (Oxford: Oxford University Press).

Kavka, M. and A. West (2004) 'Temporalities of the Real: Conceptualising Time in Reality TV', in S. Homes and D. Jermyn (eds) *Understanding Reality Television* (London and New York: Routledge).

Körner, S. (1955) *Kant* (New Haven, CT: Yale University Press).

Lury, K. (2005) *Interpreting Television* (London: Hodder Arnold).

Manvell, R. (ed.) (1972) *The International Encyclopedia of Film* (London: Michael Joseph).

Marriott, S. (2007) *Live Television: Time, Space and the Broadcast Event* (London: Sage Publications).

Montgomery, M. (2006) 'Broadcast News, the Live "Two-way" and the Case of Andrew Gilligan', *Media, Culture and Society* vol. 28 no. 2, pp. 233–59.

Nyre, L. (2008) *Sound Media: From Live Journalism to Music Recording* (London and New York: Routledge).

Ong, W. (1982) *Orality and Literacy: The Technologizing of the Word* (London and New York: Methuen).

Parker, D. (1977) *Radio: The Great Years* (Newton Abbot: David and Charles).

Pegg, M. (1983) *Broadcasting and Society, 1918–1939* (London and Canberra: Croom Helm).

Pennington, A. (2010) 'Will We All Be Watching TV Online in 2020?', *Media Guardian 'Viewing the Future' Supplement*, 1 March.

Phelan, P. (1993) *Unmarked: The Politics of Performance* (London and New York: Routledge).

Roberts, G. (2006) 'Television and DVD', in D. Gomery and L. Hockley (eds) *Television Industries* (London: BFI).

Rudin, R. (2011) *Broadcasting in the 21st Century* (Basingstoke: Palgrave Macmillan).

Sabbagh, D. (2011) 'Hollywood in Turmoil as DVD Sales Drop and Downloads Steal the Show', *Guardian*, 4 May.

Scannell, P. (1986) '"The Stuff of Radio": Developments in Radio Features and Documentaries before the War', in J. Corner (ed.) *Documentary and the Mass Media* (London: Edward Arnold).

—— (1996) *Radio, Television and Modern Life* (Oxford: Basil Blackwell).

—— (ed.) (1991) *Broadcast Talk* (London: Sage Publications).

Street, S. (2002) *A Concise History of British Radio, 1922–2002* (Tiverton: Kelly Publications).

Thompson, J. (1995) *The Media and Modernity* (Cambridge: Polity Press).

Tomlinson, J. (2007) *The Culture of Speed: The Coming of Immediacy* (London: Sage Publications).

Turow, J. (1999) *Media Today: An Introduction to Mass Communication* (Boston, MA and New York: Houghton Mifflin).

Whannel, G. (1992) *Fields in Vision: Television Sport and Cultural Transformation* (London and New York: Routledge).

Williams, K. (1998) *Get Me a Murder a Day!: A History of Mass Communication in Britain* (London: Arnold).

Williams, R. (1974) *Television: Technology and Cultural Form* (Glasgow: Fontana).

Winston, B. (1998) *Media Technology and Society* (London and New York: Routledge).

Index